U0129282

山 居 歲 月

林 明 理 著 · 吳　　　鈞 譯

Writer :Lin Mingli　　Translator: Wu Jun

文史哲英譯叢刊

文史哲出版社印行

國家圖書館出版品預行編目資料

山居歲月 / 林明理著；吳鈞譯. -- 初版 --臺
北市：文史哲，民 104.04
　　頁；公分（文史哲英譯叢刊；4）
中英對照
ISBN 978-986-314-252-2（平裝）

851.486　　　　　　　　　　104004894

文史哲英譯叢刊　　4

山　居　歲　月

著　　　者：林　　　明　　　理
譯　　　者：吳　　　　　　　鈞
出　版　者：文　史　哲　出　版　社
　　　　　　http://www.lapen.com.tw
　　　　　　e-mail：lapen@ms74.hinet.net
登記證字號：行政院新聞局版臺業字五三三七號
發　行　人：彭　　　正　　　雄
發　行　所：文　史　哲　出　版　社
印　刷　者：文　史　哲　出　版　社
臺北市羅斯福路一段七十二巷四號
郵政劃撥帳號：一六一八〇一七五
電話886-2-23511028・傳真886-2-23965656

實價新臺幣五二〇元

中華民國一〇四年（2015）四月初版

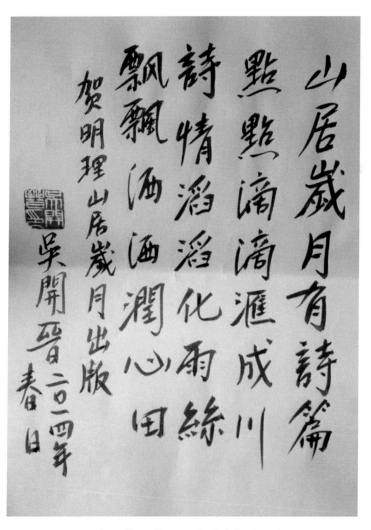

山居歲月有詩篇
點點滴滴滙成川
詩情滔滔化雨絲
飄飄洒洒潤心田

賀明理山居歲月出版

吳開晉　二〇一四年春日

山東大學文學院　吳開晉教授題勉詞

山中清晨

你當然沒見过
從鳥鳴中升起
这個屬于今天的
靜謐世界

每道光
都明亮燦爛
每次愛
都是初戀

喜見明理
山居歲月出版

非馬
2015年2月于芝加哥

美國著名非馬詩人馬為義博士題詩給明理詩人 2015.02.16

MORNING IN THE MOUNTAINS

-- for Ming-Li on her publication of
DAYS IN THE MOUNTAINS

YOU HAVE NEVER SEEN
　　SUCH A FRESH WORLD
RISING FROM BIRDSONGS
　　IN SUCH A FINE MORNING

EVERY RAY OF LIGHT
　　BRILLIANT AND DAZZLING
EACH LOVE
　　THE FIRST LOVE

給詩人非馬（馬為義博士）

林　明　理

我認得出，你是繆斯之子
偶爾，閉上眼睛
我會聽到
在世界的邊沿
你那小小的詩篇
在我耳畔鳴響
如朗照的松冠

2015.2.27

To Poet Fei Ma

(Dr. William Marr)

I can recognize, you are the son of the Muses
sometimes, when I close my eyes
I can hear
at the edge of the world
your little poems
resounding
like the brilliant pine crowns

給詩人非馬（馬為義博士）

　　　　　　　　　　杜國清

我認得出，你是繆斯之子
偶爾，闔上眼睛
我會聽到
在世界的邊陲
你那小小的詩篇
在我耳畔鳴響
如朗照的松冠

　　　　　　　　2015.2.17
　　　　　　　　于台灣
　　　　　　　　Ming-Lai

國 家 圖 書 館
NATIONAL CENTRAL LIBRARY
20,Chungshan S. Rd., Taipei Taiwan, R.O.C. 100-01
Tel:(02)2361-9132　Fax:(02)2311-0155

明理女史道鑒：

　　閣下筆耕不綴，或詩作或散文，或詩評或藝評，成章無數，著作等身，又工水彩、粉彩畫作，或山水或人物，無不深刻精妙，廣為世人所景仰。承蒙

惠贈手稿畫作，彌足珍貴，隆情高誼，無任銘感，本館自當妥善珍藏，以保文化傳承並嘉惠讀者欣賞。本館職司國家最高典藏，任重道遠，各項服務工作，尚祈　閣下不吝時賜教誨，以匡未逮。謹肅蕪箋，特申謝忱。耑此

　　敬頌

時　綏

　　　　　　國家圖書館館長　曾淑賢　　敬啟

　　　　　　　　　　民國 101　年 4 月 30 日

臺灣·「國家圖書館」館長曾淑賢博士謝函

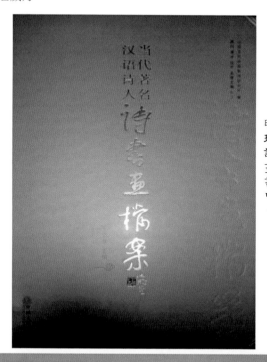

《當代著名漢語詩人詩書畫檔案》由書法家沈鵬教授題字，並收錄林明理詩畫書書中。

《当代著名汉语诗人诗书画档案》编委会

顾　　　问	屠岸	旭宇				
名 誉 主 编	牛汉					
编委会主任	马晋乾					
编委会副主任	吴开晋	李杜	鲁宏庆			
编　　　委	马青山	马林帆	马晋乾	马新朝	王玉树	王立世	王爱红
	王耀明	韦其麟	牛放	毛翰	叶文福	叶光寒	白渔
	台客	次仁罗布	牟心海	杨子忱	李发模	李杜	李芳宇
	吴开晋	辛牧	谷未黄	张双俊	张况	张德强	张默
	阿尔泰	林明理	周涛	赵少琳	赵丽宏	聂鑫森	郭蔚球
	梦也	寇宗鄂	青荷玲子	梁上泉	鲁宏庆	谢冕	霍竹山
	蔡丽双						
主　　　编	王立世					

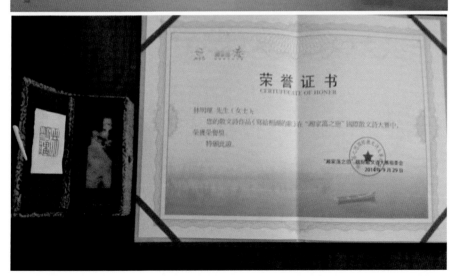

「國際散文詩」大賽獲榮譽獎

林明理、陳若曦、非馬於第 30 屆世詩會，2011.8.25 台北市

山 居 歲 月

Days in the Mountains

目 次

Contents

圖為第 22 頁〈給司馬庫斯〉插畫，刊於臺灣《人間福報》副刊 2012.11.12。

1. 給司馬庫斯

當紅柿和水蜜桃圓熟時
你和族民帶領著旅客
用累累的小米
綴滿屋前月光的篝火
讓香味流向花朵
讓濃濃鄉愁透進心中
讓曾經有過的風雨不再肆虐
讓讚美的詩歌一次一次
填滿祖靈的舊巢

啊，司馬庫斯
誰不經常看見你伴著柳杉
在上帝的園裡把你找到
在狩獵裡隨著深谷的風輕飄
有時，你倒臥在檜林
有時，你起舞在溪旁
像這秋日
隨意坐在田埂上
耐心地瞧那徐徐回家的老農

1. To Smangus

When persimmons and honey peaches are ripe
You and your folks guide the travellers
Studded the bonfire
Of moonlight in front of the house with millets
Let the frangrance flowing to the flowers
Let the thick nostalgia soaked into the hearts
Let the once willful wind and rain no longer indulge
Let the laudatory poems once more
Fill the old houses of the ancestors

Ah, Smangus
Who among us would not see you by the Japanese cedar
and find you in God's garden
Drifting with wind in deep valley while you hunt
Sometimes, you lie down under the Cypress tree
Sometimes, you dance by the brook
Like the autumn day
Sit down on the ridge of the fields at will
Looking at the old farmer going home quietly

Ah, Smangus
Children here need no fluorescent lamps
bookbags and air-conditioners
Raising their curious faces they ask
Where could we find our ancestors?
Whenever bells kocked the historical circumfluence
This time, under the Milky Way

啊，司馬庫斯
這裡孩童不需日光燈、書包和空調
他們一臉好奇，祖靈哪裡去了？
每當鐘聲將歷史回流叩響
這時啊，天河下
萬蟲寂寂，叢飛的鳥群起呼哨
群山在風裡默默祈禱
而遲歸的旅人啊
為何你也在窗前眼熱心焦？

　　註：司馬庫斯（Smangus），是臺灣新竹縣尖石鄉的部落。在泰雅語指的是一種櫟，這種高山櫟普遍生長在現今司馬庫斯、新光、鎮西堡山區。馬里闊丸群部分的先祖到此定居時，第一眼所見盡是 Smangus 樹，便以此命名。其地名延伸意即「櫟樹茂密，獵物豐厚、土壤肥沃之地！」但因位於雪山山脈主棱的山腰深處，面朝塔克金溪溪谷，海拔約一千五百公尺，早期曾被稱為「黑色部落」；後因一九九一年司馬庫斯神木群被發現，遂成為當地觀光景點。

　　直至一九七九年，司馬庫斯才有電力供應，對外道路則到一九九五年才全部修築完成；在此之前，當地居民必須徒步穿越溪穀，約莫五小時才能到相隔一個山谷的新光部落，來取得日常所需的物資以及上學。也因為地域深僻，路蜿蜒顛簸，迄今仍保留不少泰雅族的傳統生活風貌。

　　目前，部落採以「合作共生，土地共有」的農場經營模式。據林務局資料，臺灣第二名及第三名的神木都位於司馬庫斯神木區，而這兩棵司馬庫斯的神木都屬於紅檜。

── 2012.9.8 作
── 臺灣《文學臺灣》第 85 期，2013.01 春季號

Ah, Smangus
Children here need no fluorescent lamps
bookbags and air-conditioners
Raising their curious faces they ask
Where could we find our ancestors?
Whenever bells kocked the historical circumfluence
This time, under the Milky Way
All insects silent, birds whistling
Mountains are praying in the wind
But the lingering travelers
Why are you also sulking by the window?

Smangus is the name of a tribe of Jianshi village, Xinzhu County in Taiwan. In Atayal language, it refers to a kind of sawtooth oak tree. The high-mountain oak trees generally grow in the mountain areas of Smangus, Xinguang and Cinsbu nowadays. When parts of Malikoan ancestors settled here, there were all Smangus trees at their first glance, so they named their tribe after the tree. The extended meaning of this name refers to a place with dense oak trees, abundant quarries and fertile land. Because the tribe was located on the main ridge of snowy mountains and in the depths of the mountainside, facing Takejin River Valley, about 1,500 meters above sea level, it was once called "Black Tribe" during the early period; later in 1991, Smangus holy trees were found here and became a local sightseeing spot ever since.

It was not until 1979 electricity power supply was used in Smangus. The roads connected to the outside world were not completed until 1995. Before this　it took the local residents about 5 hours to walk through the valley to reach Xinguang tribe where they got the daily supplies and sent their children to school. Also because of the deeply secluded mountain area and the winding, bumpy roads, it still retains many traditional life styles of Atayal even nowadays.

Currently, the tribe adopted a management pattern of "cooperation for common existence,　cultivation of the joint land". According to the report　from the Forestry Bureau, the second and the third　holy tree were both located in Smangus tree area, both of these trees belong to red cypress.

2. 寂靜蔭綠的雪道中

在寂靜蔭綠的雪道中
風偷走了我的夢
它像小冠花對晶瑩的樹
把我心弦拋向雲層
這是怎樣的命運？無論
何處，都無法當成一首歌
在我褪去所有光輝的一刻
生命已無所求
啊⋯⋯孤寂的十月
彷彿能看到你詩思篇篇
你是我懵懂歲月的樂聲
夜裡的海洋、聖壇的明燭
爾後，我將忘卻我的驕傲
在你轉身時綻出一絲焦灼
溶入花傘下
驟然聚凝的蒼穹

— 2010.10.19
— 臺灣《秋水》詩刊，第 152 期，
　2012.01 春季號，頁 52。

2. On the Lonely Shaded Snowy Road

On the lonely shaded snowy road
My dream was stolen by the wind
Like the little crownvetch flower for the glittering tree
Throwing my heart to the clouds
What kind of fate ? Anyway
Wherever, it can not be taken as a song.
When I faded all my glory at that moment
Nothing will be desired anymore
Ah……the lonely October
I seem to see your pieces of poetic thinking.
You are the music in my innocent age
The sea of the night, the candle on the altar
Thereafter, I will forget my pride.
I'll burst out a slice of anxiety when you turn round
Dissolving into the curdled welkin
Under your colorful umbrella

3. 森林之歌

森林檜木群
整夜在雪地裡
吟唱著一首老歌

花精靈編織祖傳的故事
穿過了永恆
如幻似真

群雀及松鼠聚集在
野葛，山櫻桃，小丘的腹部。
都準備好了嗎
—— 接你們的馬車在這兒

而我輕輕地跳過柵欄
……輕輕地跳過
純屬玩笑的愛情皴裂之痛

—— 2011.1.25
—— 美國《新大陸》詩刊，第 128 期，
2012.02，頁 5。

3. Song of the Forests

Troops of cypress trees
Stand In the snow the whole night
Singing a piece of ancient song

Fairies of flowers weave an old story
Through the timeless dreamy eternity

Squirrels and sparrows gather around the bellies
Of　kudzus, mountain cherries, and small hills
Are you all ready
------the coach for you is already here

Yet I gently jump over the railings
------ gently jump
Over the spliting pain of the love of a joke

4. 風滾草

在飄泊中
在大風裡
我看到一條寂寞的
河流
推醒流沙
穿過半折裂的樹
一叢風滾草
像朝聖者般
呼喊
聲音隱秘又低沉
閃光吐焰之處　不斷
傳來草原鳴啼的歌聲

—— 2010.5.28
—— 臺灣《海星》詩刊，第 3 期，2012.03

4. Tumbleweed

In roaming
In gale
I see a lonely
River stream
Push the quicksand awake
Through the half-split tree
A cluster of grass of rolling wind
Like a pilgrim
Yelling and whooping
Secret and low and deep
Flashing and flaring, go on moving
The echoing of songs of grassland

5. 冬 日

臘冬，白雨霏霏
我走出長巷，
風，藏在桉樹林裡
神秘而狂莽
黑色枝椏上的新葉
正注視著我
像個奇幻的修士。
我偷眼望去，才片刻
已不見雨痕；
而熟悉的咖啡店前
昏黃的燈光似寂寞的小孩。

　　── 2011.9.19
　　── 刊美國《新大陸》詩刊，第 133 期，2012.12
　　── 刊臺灣《新地文學》季刊，第 22 期，2012.12

5. Winter Days

December, the white snow and rain
I walk out of the long lane
Wind, hidden among the eucalyptus trees
Mysterious and wild
The shoots of the black branches
Looking at me
Like a fantastic monk
I peek out, only a moment
The trace of the rain has gone
Yet in front of the familiar café
The light of the dusk like a lonely child

6. 思念的雨後

我
是一塊擠滿海鳥的礁岩
多渴望
看到鳥踏石仔村的雲天
如今遠眺東堤的白燈塔
已被翻頹在炸藥下隔絕了一切

那唯一的愛人啊
已過了這麼多年頭的變遷
我抑制無用的激情和悲哀的潮水
只想再看一次噶瑪蘭〈Kavalan〉失落的前院
想那昔日捕飛魚的人兒
是否已忘了我？任我孤單
想那歌舞喧嘩，田田心事
我就知道今年來得並不太遲
在冰冷的海岸邊
那祖靈也個個望盡深處
即便如此，我仍不由自主地來到你跟前

6. *Missing After the Rain*

I am
A reef rock crowded with seabirds
How I wish to see
Clouds and sky above Birds- filled- Shizai village
Look at the white lighthouse on east bank afar
Already ruins isolated from all by the explosion

Ah, my only love
Already changes for so many years
I control my useless passion and mournful tidewater
Once more a look for the lost forecourt of Kavalan
Recalling of him who caught the volador in the past
Do you still remember me ? Leave me here lonely
Remember hustling songs and dances, full of worries
Then I know I come here not late this year
By the icy seashore
Ancestors were also looking and expecting
Even so
I could not keep my steps from coming to you

別說
再沒有那最神聖的痛苦焚胸或連星兒也
不敢淚漣
如今，雨聲過後，山雀依然入林
月光盤踞不走
而你是否靜靜睡著，不再長歎？

註：花蓮港所在地以前的地名是「鳥踏石仔村」，村裡有一塊大礁石，
在花蓮築港以前，礁石上常有海鳥群集。白燈塔建於 1939 年，古樸
的白色水泥圓柱造型。因為第四期拓港工程展開，白燈塔於 1980 年
6 月已不復見。

—— 2011.10.30
—— 臺灣《笠》詩刊，第 289 期，
2012.06.15

Don't say

No more the most divine pains burning, or the stars

Dare not to shed tears

Now, after the rain, tits still fly into the woods

Moonlight still shines

If you still sleep sound, no more deep signs?

7. 惦 念

整個冬天
雪從沙路上銜起了
啼聲
春天
你是霧中羊
把我的回憶
搖成咽啞的頸鈴

遠方
綿綿山巒
拉曳出點點星辰
有棵樹仍挺立
慢慢
消融了我瘦骨的影

—— 2011.1.23
—— 臺灣《海星》詩刊，第 3 期，
2012.03 春季號

7. Worries

The whole winter
Snow turns up from the sandy road
The chirping

The spring
You are a sheep in the fog shaking my memory
Into toneless bells on the neck

Far away
Long stretch of mountains Dragging out drops of stars
A tree still standing
Slowly
Melting my thin shadow

8. 夜宿南灣 (一)

哦我從細雨中
企圖在窗內漫過自己
發愣的腳步　總是輕的
那隨時可以發光的海
在睡夢裡
一條老街連接無盡
月也不動
索隱著我的暗語
我低垂著：
早已習慣在風中敘事
破霧而飛
請來點兒音樂
讓我不再想著那個望海的老人
就從這蕩漾開始吧
直唱到黎明
在枝葉間
炫目的一瞥

—— 2011.6.22
—— 臺灣《笠》詩刊，第 287 期，
　　2012.02，頁 148。

8. Night at South Bay 1

Oh, I'm from the drizzling rain
Trying to brim over myself through the window
Dazed footsteps, always slight

The sea shimmering at any time
In sleep dreams
An old street connects the endless
The moon is still
Hiding my code words

I droop down
Long time already used to tell in the wind
Break through the fog and fly

Come to give some music
let me no longer think of the old man looking at the sea
Start from the waving ripples
Singing till the dawn
Among the leaves
Casting a dazzling glance

9. 無言的讚美

我和西天
追趕不上的雲朵
踏上這一片夢土

薩摩亞的藍湖初醒
雄奇而神秘
撲眼而來

山是以沉默　露出
蘋果也似的
笑容

—— 2011.6.23 作
—— 臺灣《笠》詩刊，第 287 期，
　　2012.02，頁 150。

9. Silent Praise

The western sky and I
The clouds we can not catch up
Setting our feet on the land of dream

Awaking of the Samoa' blue lake
Imposing and mysterious
Rushing on

Mountains are silent, revealing
The smile
Like an apple

10. 啊，卡地布

要是說
巴拉冠〈註〉有一個金色的夜晚
那定是從勇士舞遊街
　發出來祖靈的呼喚
那定是熊熊篝火
　永不熄滅的愛的吶喊

它豎立起精神圖騰
每當小米收穫後
　彩色的樂音
　高揚而靈活
彩蝶般翩翩
燃燒著團聚的希望

啊卡地布，夏樹的陽光
伴隨著
　那個靦腆笑容的小孩
　身影凝聚成大鵬
無限地伸向天空
　在福爾摩莎小島上

註：台東知本原名「卡地布」，卑南族語意「在一起」或「團結」。
　　巴拉冠在台東線知本卑南族青年會所。

　　　　　　　　　—— 2011.7.18
　　　　　　　　　—— 高雄市《新文壇》季刊，2012.04 夏季號

10. Oh, Katipul

If we have to say
There is a golden night in Barak
That must be the calling of our ancestors
From the street of warriors dancing parade
That must be the blazing bonfire
The eternal whoop of passionate love

It sets up the spirit totem
Whenever after the harvest of millets
The colorful music
Soaring and floating
Like fluttering butterflies
With burning wish of reunification

Oh Katipul , sunshine for the summer trees
Along with
The shy and smiling kid
Agglomerate his body into a roc
Unlimitedly extending to the sky
In the Formosa island

11. 又是雨幕的清晨

我無法忘懷那凋萎之夜，
我無法召回潺潺的泉水，
我無法聽到那風笛
在廣場裡呼喚綣曲的聲音。

那遍插的茱萸永少一人，
你無法讓他重生。
愁雨裡的孤燈又怎能
抵得住我綿綿的思情？
年年的花祭已隨風而逝，
時間又擱淺在無言的桌前，
仲夏的驚雨喚不醒你的沉睡，
莫非你已不再理會躊躇的明天？

那風笛已經離開很遠，
遙遠天邊有星子徘徊，
徘徊在星空的天使的樂音，
也已充滿了溫柔與慈悲。

11. Again, a Drenching Rain in the Morning

I can't forget that languishing night,
I can't recall back the loquacious spring
I can't hear that skirl from the square
The echoing of calling of frizzy sound

There's always one cornel absent from the all
You are incapable to make his rebirth
How could the lonely light in the sad rain
Stop my endless thinking and longing
Year's memorial ceremony for flowers gone
Time has lingered in front of the speechless desk
Midsummer rain could not wake your sound sleep
If you don't care your hesitant tomorrow any more

The whistling sound of the bagpipe has gone far away
Stars are lingering by remote outer edge of the sky
The angelic melody echoing in the outer space
Is also filled with gentleness and mercy

昔日在寒夢中重返的尊嚴，
已站在希望之花擎起的蒼穹，
心中只剩下不熄的意念，
呵六月，逝去的你永不復歸。

— 追悼「1989 天安門事件」— 2011.06
— 臺灣《乾坤》詩刊，第 62 期，2012.04

Dignity returned yesterday from the chilly dream
Already stand under the sky held by flowers of hope
There only the unextinguished will remain
Oh, June, you the lost can't never return

12. 問 愛

在深不可測的眼神裡
我無法判斷
哪些是真實哪些是謊言

籃子裡的貓，瞇著眼
打了個呵欠
回答了所有的問題

牠懶洋洋地蹲伏於窗口
知道我無法逃遁

最後牠輕輕踱向我
彷彿愛情根本不存在過
除了這晦暗的雨中寧靜

—— 2011.1.16
—— 臺灣《乾坤》詩刊，第 62 期，
2012.04

12. Question of Love

In the unfathomable eyes
I can't judge
Which is the truth and which the false

The cat in the basket, narrows its eyes
Yawning
Answered all the questions

It crouches lazily by the window
Knowing that I can't escape

Finally it walks up to me
As if love never existed
Except the tranquility in the gloomy rain

13. 歌飛霍山茶鄉

一、

三月西山穀雨後
古林寺前
群雀及松鼠聚集在
瓊花、芍藥、雨花臺的周邊
但我卻輕輕地
想起你
彷彿還在金竹坪上山坡
風兒帶著你的溫暖
帶著你的愛
再將茶香
斟滿我幸福的心房

看哪，那桃源雲兒撩撥著
三千歲月
將霍山老農
以熟板栗香
送掛著一畦畦嫩勻的綠與

13. Songs Flying in Tea Country of Huo Mountain

Part 1
After Grain Rain day in March on Western Hill
Before the temple of ancient forest
Sparrows and squirrels gather
By guelder roses, peonies,
and Terrace of Rain flowers
I remind you quietly
As if I still on the slope of Jinzhuping hillside
Wind brings your warm and love
Along with the fragrant tea
Pouring happiness to my heart fully

Look, peach blossoms sprinkling
Three thousand yeas
Offer the old farmer of the Huoshan Mountain
Savory cooked chestnut
Hanging layers of tender green farmland
With blinking and shining sweat

閃光的汗
南鄉之霧已在我腳下了
忽有清明的炒茶聲催促我
從初烘到足火
踩筒的動作
一如春風吹開花萬朵

金陽下，佛子嶺水庫上的天真
像是幻覺
整片茶林
磅礡的綠
漂浮在欸乃間
一種聲音
猶如棕雀，在斜暉脈脈時
響起 ——
霍山黃何以如此美麗
我信步在霧林裡
那拖曳的星辰也不時柔聲絮語

聽哪，烏米尖及掛龍尖山
那一片不變的茶園
在朦朧的月色中

The mist of Nanxiang country was under my feet
When the clear voice of frying tea was echoing
From the first baking to the full firing
The action of stepping on the bamboo canisters
Like spring breeze blowing open flowers

In the golden sunlight
The purity above the reservoir of Foziling
Like a fantasy
The whole tea grove
A billowing green
Floating in the sound of singing while oaring
A voice
Seemed from a brown sparrow, in setting sunlight
Chirping
The yellow color of Huoshan Mountain so beautiful
I strolled in the foggy forest
Listening to the whispers of the daggling stars

Listen, Mountains of Wumijian and Gualongjian
Among the unchanged stretch of tea garden
In the hazymoonlight
I heard from the dark of stars

聆聽星的驛站
輾轉傳來
你欣逢的迴響
春風太早，藏在我的衣袖
你的身影悄悄浮現
前方有窗櫺在叮叮地響
響起的名字也仍舊是大別山北麓的
樹與群星齊舞的足音

彷彿中
我聽見了老山泉在金雞山東轉
一隻歸雁在煙波細雨裡
急急緩緩　往重岩迭嶂行
那太陽河、漫水河和石羊河仍悠悠地流
牢繫著古城的倒影
每當我思念時即為兩岸的分隔而愁悵
啊，這才想起
那黃山毛峰、六安瓜片、太平猴魁還有
祁門紅茶和霍山黃芽（註）
原停泊在離我不遠的路徑上

二、
在大別山上

Your happy and joyously echoes
Spring breeze was too early, hidden in my sleeves Your
figure quietly emerged
In front of me, tinkling window lattice
Echoing the ringing names of northern hill slope
Sound of steps of dancing of trees and stars
of Dabie Mountain

In my fantasy, as if,
I hear old spring
rotating in the east of Jinji Mountain
A wild goose flying among mist and drizzle
Hurriedly or slowly, for the ranges of mountains
Sun River, Overflowing River and Shiyang River
Still leisurely flowing
Firmly tied to the reflection of the ancient town
Whenever I miss my home
I'm worry about the separation of the river bank
Then I remind
Maofeng Tea from Huangshan Mountain
Lu'an Melon Seed tea, Taiping Houkui Tea and Keemun Black Tea
and Huo Mountain Yellow Bud Tea
Staying not far from me on the road

Part 2
In the Dabie Mountain

點點白鷺，振翅了
在茶畝
旋舞如縷煙
那諸佛庵鎮金家灣
眾山動容
在靜謐花香的萬佛湖
壽縣古城和天堂寨上
它們慢條斯理地望我
霎時間，夢中的翅膀也飛入八公山
停泊在楚文化博物館

看哪，那灼灼星光在彼岸閃爍
近在咫尺的你
以沉定的力量
坐臥於六安市的夜晚
我在霧中等待
等待朝陽依然徐徐爬上金山頭
那些專家和廠商齊力把一度失傳的茶技
從重新開始研製到恢復生產
以忠實，以熟板栗香
讓霍山黃芽站上世界舞臺
讓古代的貢茶成了奧運之光

In the tea Several egrets, fluttering their wings
field
Circling like thread of smoke
Nunneries and temples of Jinjiawan town
All mountains in emotion
In the quiet Wanfo lake with fragrance of flowers
From old town of Shouxian and Tiantang village
They looked at me leisurely
Instantly, dreams flew to Bagong Mountain
Anchoring at the Museum of Chu culture

Look, the twinkling stars above the other shore
Near at hand of you
with the calm power
Sitting in the night of LiuAn city
I wait in the fog
waiting for the morning sun rises
Slowly to the top of the golden hill
Experts and manufacturers work together
To recover the skill of tea-making that once lost
From the research to the production
with Loyalty, with the savories of cooked chestnuts
Tea of Huo Mountain Yellow Buds appear
The ancient tribute tea became the light of Olympic

到如今
我不知道
這南鄉之霧
是否還是盪氣迴腸
一壺老茶，沏著舊時光
我不知道
那記憶的河水　是否還是靜靜流淌
今夜舊街巷，光芒或淡黯
我不知道
那夢裡的茶鄉　是否還是舉杯邀月
對影共桂香

一枝綠柳
銜來一個春天
把難以揣測的大地吻醒
每當我徜徉在群山
像葉脈裡的蟬
那紅日親四吻田水
茶歌再起的時候
且讓群雀銜接飄泊
讓思想再度飛旋著

Up till now
I don't know
Whether the Southern Fog
Is still soul-stirring
A pot of traditional tea, brews the old time
I don't know
Whether the current of memory
Is still quietly flowing
Tonight the old streets and alleys, bright or dim
I don't know
Whether the men in the tea country of my dream
Are still inviting the moon to drink together
With double shadows and fragrant laurels

A green willow
Brings a spring
kisses the elusive earth awake
Whenever I wander about in the mountains
Like a cicada in the veins of leaves
The sun kisses the water in the paddy field
When the songs of tea arise again
Let the sparrows fly freely
Let the thoughts revolve again

啊，歌飛

茶鄉 ——

啊，我們謳歌

我們啜飲綠野

那香氣鮮爽

全憑葉低黃亮，味雅回甘

雲不曾改變其顏色

我的思念也未曾停歇

在山居月下

與夜一起奔跑的季節裡

在蟲鳥唧唧鳴鳴的陽光裡

啊，那霍山勞動人民的笑靨

是如此淨潔，如此真切，叫人難忘

註：《史記》記載：壽春之山有黃芽焉，可煮而飲，久服得仙。六霍舊
　　壽春故也。一曰仙芽，又稱壽州霍山黃芽。唐楊曄《膳夫經手金錄》
　　載："有壽州霍山小團，此可能仿造小片龍芽作為貢品，其數甚微，
　　古稱霍山黃，芽乃取一旗一槍，古人描述其狀如甲片，葉軟如蟬翼，
　　是未經壓制之散茶也。"

—— 2012.1.4 作

—— 獲安徽省六安市宣傳部主辦
　　「霍山黃茶」杯全國原創
　　詩歌大賽組委會「榮譽獎」
　　榮譽證書於 2012.4.21。

Ah, songs soaring
My tea county----

Ah, we sing the praise songs
We sip the green wildness
The fresh and cool air
All comes from the bright yellow leaves low
And elegant and fragrant flavour
Clouds never change its color
My thoughts never stop
In the mountain under the moon
In the season when running with the night
In the sunshine when birds and worms chirping
Ah, the smile of people in Huoshan Mountain
So clean, so real, so unforgettable

Note:

According to Shiji （Historical Records）, there are yellow buds in Shouchun Mountain, which can be cooked for drinking tea. If you drink it often, you will become a fairy. That is the reason why Liuhuo is called Shouchun （ with the meaning of long live） in the old days. One kind of it is called fairy buds, also known as yellow buds of Huoshan of Shou state. According to "Golden Record of Chef" which was written by Yangye in Tang dynasty, "there are small rolls of tea from Huo Mountain of Shou state which can imitate little pieces of dragon buds as a tribute, and it is very precious and with very small quantity. In the ancient time it was called Huoshan Yellow. The tea leave likes one flag and one spear putting together. In the old time people described the buds as sclerites, the tea leaves soft as the wings of cicadas. It is a kind of well known unsuppressed loose tea.

14. 吉貝耍‧孝海祭

每年農曆九月初五
牽曲後，在風中
我們沿著農路
佇立在黃昏盡頭
時間悄悄地過去
草蟲嗚嗚
黑夜之手正縫補著歷史的傷口

但是這夜祭的時刻，是什麼讓你煩憂著
什麼在給那苦難的地土吹奏？
也許
每當澤蘭放進祀壺而木棉開滿部落
我們又回到西拉雅〈Siraya〉
看陽光逐漸黯淡
看族民如何努力生活
畫出了東河村一片富足
看這雨後的寧靜
把耆老的夢拋向更遠的夜的懷抱……

14. Kapasau.Mourning Marine Sacrifice

Each year on the fifth of September of lunar calendar
After the ritual dance, in the wind
We walk along the country road
Stand at the end of the nightfall
Time passed quietly
Insects buzz and chirp around
The hands of Night are mending the wound of history

But what is bothering you in the moment of sacrifice
What is playing for the land of suffering
Perhaps
Every time when herba lycopi are put in the pot
And kapoks are in blooms all over the tribe
We go back again to Siraya
Watching the sun setting gradually
Observing the clan's hard life
Drawing up the picture of richness of East River Village
And the serenity after the rain
Throw the old dream far away to the embrace of night

遠遠地
我聽見了古老的叮嚀
那發自周遭的合鳴
使我不再感到淒苦
啊⋯⋯吉貝耍
—— 這名字
也從未消失過

註：吉貝耍孝海祭是台南縣東山鄉東河村吉貝耍平埔族的重要祭典。關於「孝海
　　祭」的由來，根據當地耆老的說法，其一，是因有許多先民渡海來台時死於
　　海上，所以，每年在大公廨附近的農田，面向西南方大海的方向，遙拜祖靈，
　　以示不忘祖。其二，為當初祖先渡海來台，曾受當地一位漁民「阿海」接濟，
　　引導祖先從倒風內海到蕭壟登陸。之後，阿海在某年的農曆九月初五於魚塭
　　遭雷殛身亡，蕭壟社民感念其恩情，族人搬遷至吉貝耍後，因感懷海祖恩澤，
　　特地在海祖仙逝日，面向大海方向祭拜他，遂而發展出「孝海」祭典。「孝
　　海祭」於農曆九月初五下午兩點左右舉行，吉貝耍人陸續擔著飯菜到大公廨
　　西南方農路上，排列在農路兩旁，以祭品來答謝祖靈。祭司到祭壇前「三向」
　　（西拉雅語，祭拜的儀式名詞），三向畢，祭司拿起烓祖拐、澤蘭葉（西拉
　　雅祭司法器）口含米酒噴向空中，請祖靈、海祖來看「海戲」，並且接受子
　　民們的祭品。這時「牽曲」婦女以西拉雅母語吟唱，也圍繞著祭壇祀壺，以
　　表達對祖靈眷顧之恩。在助理祭司的指示下，族人將甘蔗葉插入酒瓶中，不
　　久祭司就代表祖靈一一巡視村人擺設的祭品飯菜。祖靈若歡喜點收子民心
　　意，祭司則下令由助手逐一把插在祭品酒瓶上的蔗葉拔去，「戳酒洞」畢，
　　表示祭典即將告一段落，祭司回到祭壇以剖半檳榔為擲筊，請示祖靈，「聖
　　栖」後，牽曲才可停止；族人收拾飯菜後，「孝海祭」就畫上句點。

—— 2012.5.19 作
—— 原載臺灣《文學臺灣》季刊，第 83 期，
　　2012.07 秋季號。
—— 轉載真理大學臺灣文學資料館《臺灣文學評論》，
　　第 12 卷第 3 期，2012.07.15。

Afar

I heard the ancient advises

The chorus rose from all around

I then felt no more of sadness

Oh ……Kapasau

---the name

That had never passed

Note:

Mourning Marine Sacrifice of Kapasau is an important sacrificial ceremony of Pingpu clan of Kapasau. The origin of "Mourning Marine Sacrifice", according to the elderly locals, comes from the old lengend that, for one saying, many ancestors died at sea when they were crossing the sea to Taiwan. So, every year to remember the ancestors the offspring of the pioneers worship them toward the southwest sea in their farmland near Dagongxie. Another saying goes like this: when the ancestors were crossing the sea to Taiwan a local fisherman named Ah Hai helped them. He led the ancestors land at Xiao Long from the inner sea to Daofeng lagoon. Later, Ah Hai died of lightning in fish pond on fifth of September of Chinese lunar calendar. People from XiaoLong always remember Ah Hai's kindness and after the ancestors moved to Kapasau, they worshiped him every year on the day of his death. They made worships toward the sea , and gradually this ceremony developed into the Mourning Marine Sacrifice . The ceremony is held at two o'clock in the afternoon of the fifth of September of Chinese lunar calendar every year.

15. 夏之吟

客自光影中來，可曾見某個驛站

有海濤回音，唯抒出了

這一季沉思中的

牧笛歡響 ——

好似一瞬間

天空失去了體重

被空氣托舉著

啊灼人的夜，青禾的吻落在小羊兒夢上

—— 2011.12.16
—— 臺灣《海星》詩刊，第 5 期，
2012.09 秋季號

15. Summer Songs

From the light shadow he comes
If he once saw a dak somewhere there
The sea waves are echoing with
The contemplation of this season
Reed pipes utter merry sounds
It seems just　a moment
The sky has lost its weight
And　is raised by the air
Ah , scorching night
The kisses of green crops are falling
On the dreams of the little lamb

16. 海 頌

穿過雲霧
我看見佛光在金頂
在高樓、在海面
每遇
七零八碎的破瓶兒
便把自己螺貝的耳殼
高懸半空
傾聽聲聲嗚咽

　　　　　── 2011.12.23
　　　　　── 臺灣《海星》詩刊，第 5 期，
　　　　　　　2012.09 秋季號
　　　　　── 收錄譚五昌教授編「國際漢語詩歌」，
　　　　　　　2013.11，頁 186，北京，線裝書局出版。

16. Ode of the Sea

Through the clouds
I see the light of Buddha on the golden top
On the high tower, on the sea level
Whenever I encounter
The broken bottles with bits and pieces
I'll hang my spiral- shell- like ears
In the mid-air
Listening to the sound of sobbing

17.夕陽，驀地沉落了

夕陽，驀地沉落了
在魚鱗瓦上
在老厝的茶園旁
一片灰雲
躲入我衫袖

時常跟著我
一步步奔躍向前的
小河
加快了步子
臨近新丘

就這樣
從河而來
翻飛的記憶
恰似風鈴花開
雖然披紅那堪早落

—— 2012.5.10 作
—— 臺灣《人間福報》副刊刊登圖文，
2012.06.05

17 The setting sun, suddenly sank down

The setting sun, suddenly sinks down
On the scale tiles
By the old teahouse
A gray cloud
hides in my sleeves

Always follows me
Jumps and moves forward
The brook
Quickens his steps
Aproachhing the new hillock

Thus
Coming from the river
With the waving memories
Like the blooms of campanulas
Though still wrapped in red
But can't stand the early decline

18. 魯花樹

這裡是冬天
巷內的魯花樹下
　一尊木刻神像
展顏於金晃晃的葉縫間
那闇影，多麼安靜，使我入睡
鮮麗的漿果
　　由綠　而黃　而紅
織就了無數個童年
　　而我視線之下
從未感到如此純淨
每當風神前來糾纏
　　枝上歌雀齊集鳴飛
它便伸長脖頸
將往來的面孔、昆蟲或遠自
祖靈的呼喚，都一一收藏

註：魯花樹據說是花東地區原住民語的音譯，原住民取其樹幹為搗小米
　　用的杵，排灣族以其根莖做黑褐色的染料。

—— 2011.8.21 作
—— 香港《橄欖葉》詩報，第 3 期，
2012.06

18. Scolopia Tree

Here it is already winter
In the alley under the Scolopia Tree
A woodcut statue of a god
Shines with golden light among the leaves
The shadow is quiet, making me fall asleep

Fresh and pretty berries
From green to yellow to red
Waving countless dreams of childhood
I have never felt so pure

Whenever the God of wind comes to entwine
Singing birds gathered to chirp on the branches
Then he stretches his neck
Putting all the faces, insects or the
distant Calling of the ancestors, into his bag

19. 在淺溪邊的茵綠角落裡

我心隱痛，如清溪
細細諦聽無花果樹的剝落。
即使沒有綿羊牧童，偶爾
飛花鳴蛩，直到不自覺地沉湛其中。

到底生命的源頭，是否
來自無窮的底洞？
那迴盪於芳草間的歌雀
是否也曾飛躍千重？

噢，親愛的，那星子的深婉
如你沈鬱而焦慮的瞳孔
似乎召喚我，就像這冷杉
端立於恒常的夜空。

—— 2010.5.30
—— 美國《新大陸》詩刊，第 130 期，
2012.06

19. In the Gloomy Corner by the Brook

My heart secretly anguishes, like clear brook
Listen carefully the peeling away of the fig tree
Even without sheep and cowboy, occasionally
Flying petals and chirping crickets
Until unconsciously obsessed in it

Anyway the origin of life , if
It is originated from the bottom of infinity hole
Whether the sparrow leaping on green grass
Once has passed over thousand miles.

Oh, my dear, the depth of the star
Like your blue and anxious pupils
As if to call for me , like this fir
Standing still under the eternal night sky

20. 夜宿南灣 (二)

哦我從密雨中
傾聽著，白窗外的椰林：
夜如同貓眼般
如此沉寂，如此神秘，如此吞吸著
我那過度焦慮的折磨
儘管如此
黎明仍偎在山梁
而沙灘的足音
即將消逝
在汪海裡
在太空裡
在許我太多的幸福的
暮色

—〈2011.02.25 夜宿墾丁有感〉
—2011.3.1 作
—美國《新大陸》詩刊，第 130 期，2012.06

20. Night at Southern Bay 2

Oh! I 'm through the dense rain
Listening, the coconut trees by the white window:
The night was like a cat's eye
So quiet, so mysterious, so swallowing
My excessively exhausted torture
Nevertheless
The dawn still nestles in the ridge of the mountain
The footsteps sound on the sand
Vanishing
In the boundless sea
In the vast outer space
In the twilight
Promised too much happiness to me

21. 秋之楓

入夜
深谷裡
一棵棵楓忍住呻吟
那伸長的手臂
像雨中飛燕
拍搏著眼中長出的愁緒

—— 2011.12.18
—— 臺灣《乾坤》詩刊，第 63 期，
　　2012.07

21. Maples of Autumn

Night
Deep valley
Maples refrain from moaning.
The long stretched arms
Like swallows in the rain
Struggling against the gloominess out of the eyes

22. 玉山，我的母親

我沿著僻靜的石子路漫走
與你進行零距離親昵
即使大地沉睡如嬰
心中的力量讓我奮勇邁往 ——
一切妄念拋下
啊，金色的原野，坦露的胸膛
似母親溫柔深過海洋
多想將你緊貼我心，恒久激盪

—— 2011.12.12
—— 臺灣《乾坤》詩刊，第 63 期，
2012.07 秋季號

22. Yushan Mountain, My Mother

I walk along the quiet gravel road
Close to you from zero distance
Even if the earth sleeps like a baby
The power of the heart gives me the courage---
I throw all of my improper thoughts
Ah, golden fields, bared chest
Like Mother's gentleness of the sea
How I want to bring you close to my heart
For lasting emotional dash

23. 憶夢

哪裡去尋找
一種聲音
像枝葉間接力的蟬
在廣場前
新穀還有漸次消失的
田，老農撩起褲管
種菜插秧

啊小小的火窗
燃燒著希望
在溝岸旁
抓魚、游泳、釣蛙
油菜花和小雲雀嬉遊
街燈黯淡而溫暖

現在我知道
無論什麼季節
有一種聲音
像只蟹，眼裡還沾著細沙
就迫不及待往岸上爬
它牽引著我，在清蔭的夜晚

註：火窗又稱迷你烘爐〈火爐〉，在寒冬給老人家取暖用的。
　　── 2012.5.15 作
　　── 臺灣 真理大學《臺灣文學評論》，第 12 卷第 3 期，2012.7.15
　　── 轉載香港《橄欖葉》詩報，第 4 期第 4 版，2012.12

23. Recalling of the Dream

Where to look for
A voice
Like a relay of cicadas among the leaves
In front of the square
New grain and the gradually disappearing
Fields, the old farmer lifted his trouser legs
Growing vegetables and planting seedlings

Ah, the little fire window
With the burning hope
By the ditch
Fishing, swimming and catching frogs
Cole flowers and little larks are playing
Street lights dim and warm

Now I know
No matter what season it is
There is a voice
Like a crab , with silver sand stained on its eyes
Climb to the bank impatiently
It draughts me, in a cool and shading night

24. 森林深處

熱霧過後
老戰士依然跋涉回來
空氣中，有巴魯果氣味
一棵小肉桂樹
留下了抓痕
這定是懶熊的傑作
幾位族人都這麼說
而祖靈們也正默默思索
彷彿花豹俯瞰著自己領土
看到的是動物越來越少的死寂或
憂慮這僅存的部落

這乾旱的尖峰期
樹林卻開花了
蝴蝶離開了水窪，翩翩的薄翼閃爍晶亮
多麼輕靈，充滿夢幻
整個林子像彩虹般
它標誌，一個哲人的形象
就在今夜
為了土地變得繽紛而在那裡咿呀作響

24. Deep in the Forest

After the hot mist
The old soldier trudged back
In the air, smell of the Baruch fruits
On a small cinnamon tree
Some scratches left on
It must be the works of a sloth bear
Several clansmen all said so
Ancestral souls are also pondering
As if leopards overlook its territory
They see the deathly stillness of few animals
And worry about the only tribe remained

At the peak of drought
Trees are in bloom
Butterflies leave the puddles
Shining wings glitter
How brisk, full of fantasy
The whole woods like a rainbow
Symbolize an image of a philosopher
Tonight

為了月夜慢慢地織好了羅網
讓拂不掉的痛苦記憶
讓餵奶的母親 —— 甦醒的大地
用呼吸，從我這兒帶走莫名的憂傷

升起吧，醺醉的太陽

—— 2012.5.12
—— 臺灣 真理大學《臺灣文學評論》，
　　第 12 卷第 3 期，2012.7.15

For the fertile land it rings
For the moonlight it waves
Whisk away the unforgetable painful memory
Let the nursing mother—the awakened land
Breathingr, take away the nameless sorrow

Rises , the drunk sun

25. 追悼 ── 陳千武前輩

我願是只灰喜鵲，如果你是流浪的鞋
或許，就能聽見花瓣旋轉入林
雨滴落在碑前
昆蟲低鳴猶響

我願是只大藍鯨，如果你是海上的月
或許，在黑夜裡，在斑斕間
迎著微風如遊如飛
每當你低著頭像慈眉老人一樣審視我

── 2012.6.27
── 臺灣《笠》詩刊，第 290 期，2012.08
── 收錄《永遠的懷念，時代的鼓手 ── 陳
　　千武紀念文集》，南投縣文化局出版，
　　頁 138，2014.05

25. Mourn for Grand Old Man, Chen Qianwu

I would rather be a gray magpie
If you were a pare of wandering shoes
Or, I could hear petals whirling in the trees
Raindrops fall down in front of the stele
The low chirps are echoing

I would rather be a huge blue whale
If you are the moon on the sea
Or, in the dark night, among the gorgeous
Greeting the breeze, flying or swimming
Whenever you look at me like a kind old man

26. 山居歲月

一聲磬中洗騷魂，

　　幾點霧雨迢曉月；

杏林徑裡有孤竹，

　　晚課聲中看鳥飛。

—— 2011.12.20
—— 美國《新大陸》詩刊，第 131 期，
2012.08

26. Days in the Mountains

With the sound of chime stone I came into meditation.

In the mist and drizzle I watched the moon afar

A lonely bamboo stands in the apricot grove

With evensongs my heart follows the flying birds

此圖為二六八頁〈回鄉〉二插畫，刊於
人間福報二〇一四年十二月二日

27. 永懷鐘鼎文老師

如松影般縹緲
你的靈魂
立在深澗上
健步登天庭
雖說草聲默默
虹彩寂寂
而你溫文的眼神
如雨露，如晨星
迎接無限的陽光
從未止盡

攝影於 2009.6.19 王璞新書發表會
——臺灣「國家圖書館」

—— 2012.8.17 同悼〈鐘老師 2012.8.12
　　逝世於臺北榮民醫院，享壽百歲〉
—— 臺灣《人間福報》副刊刊登圖文，
　　2012.9.4

27. Mourn for Mr. Zhong Dingwen

As ethereal as the shadow of a pine tree
Your soul
Stands over the ravine
Walks with vigorous strides to the heaven
Although the grass is silent
Rainbow is alone
Yet your warm eyes
Like the rain , like the dew ,like the morning star
Greeting the unlimited sun
Never ending.

28. 夏風吹起的夜晚

我辭別了我故鄉的小窗
離開了我心愛的土壤。
當年禾田像新煤般
泛滿老父的顧盼。
火車似一隻灰黑的蟬
伏在靜寂的月臺上。
又如一只溫馴的小山羊——
偎依著溫暖的土壤。
何時歸來啊，已無法想像，
田野反復地跟著星辰運轉，
門前小溪一路歌唱，
窗外擴散的世界一片天藍。
呵再會吧，再會吧，故鄉的夜晚
也許，我底愛赤裸而坦蕩
偶爾有躍出來迷朦來路的月
它的容顏將再觸及我不眠的憂傷。

—— 20112.12
—— 美國《新大陸》詩刊，第 131 期，2012.08

28. Night with Summer Wind

I left my small window of my hometown
I left my beloved land
That time the cropland liked new coal
Full of the expectation of my old father

The train liked an ashy black cicada
Groveling on the platform quietly
And liked a docile little fawn
Nestling upon the warm soil

When shall I go back, already no way to think
The fields cycle repeatedly with the stars
The creek in front of the doo still murmuring along
The world out side the window is a pure blue sky

Oh, goodbye, goodbye, the night of my hometown
Maybe, my love is pure and magnanimous
Once in a way jump out to fan the rising moon
Its looks as if it'll again touch my sleepless mourn

29. 默　念

當你返身瞬間 ——
再沒有什麼可憔悴
即使
僅存在夢裡的
一絲威儀
恰如寒雁疾飛
再沒有遷徙之距

如果能夠 ——
就這樣，像那飛鷹
有鐵般靈魂
縱然
在黑暗的廣漠中
再沒有為理想而痛苦的憂愁

啊誰能找到被風帶走的
你的聲音
那顫著雪的夜呵
如果你側耳聽
它交織著我萬古常新的
目光
生怕再次打開愛的黎明

　　　—— 2012.4.28 作
　　　—— 刊臺灣《海星》詩刊，第 6 期，2012.12 冬季號

29. Silent Thought

The moment when you returned
Nothing more could be languishing
Even if
Only in the dream
A hint of dignity
Like the wild goose gliding through the cold sky
No more the distance for migration

If I can ----
Just like this, like the flying eagle
With an iron soul
Even
In the vast dark deserts
No more sorrow s of the suffering for the ideal

Oh, who can find out your voice
That was taken away by the wind
The shivering snowy night
If you are all ears
You can hear it interweaved
My eyesight
New and lasting for thousands of years
So as not to open the dawn of love again

30. 拂曉時刻

我們遇到迷霧
雖說還是冬季
湖塘微吐水氣
睫毛上也沾著露珠

細談中
一隻鷺在鏡頭前踟躕
這濕地森林
悄然褪色
萬物彷彿都在睡中

哪裡是野生天堂
如何飛離憂悒的白晝
我們啞然以對
只有小河隨心所願貌似輕鬆

　　　　　— 2012.5.11
　　　　　— 刊臺灣《海星》詩刊，第 6 期，
　　　　　　2012.12 冬季號

30. At Daybreak

We meet with dense fog
Although it's winter still
The pond gently spits up vapor
Dewdrops hang on our eyelashes

Chatting in detail
An egret is wavering before the camera lens
The wetland and forest
Fading away quietly
Everything seems to be in sleep

Where is paradise for the wild
How to fly away from the sorrowful daylight
We are mute for the answer
Only the brook seems to take it easy
Bubbling away willingly

31. 秋 林

再一次，漫步秋林，
我拾得一小隊的雁；
何曾擁有這般的感覺
—— 淒美
—— 縈回
而充滿深邃！

那白草的光，穿過幽徑，
引我從容看待一切；
一如曠野輕輕踱步的雲，
再次向你親近；
即使靈魂突然從游離裡，
俯衝向無人的溪地。

或像雪在沙路上
銜起了竹聲；
而你是低翔的歌雀，
把我僅存的記憶，
變成叼起的星辰，
與模糊的地平線相會。

31. Forest in Autumn

Once again, strolling in the autumn forest
I catch up with a line of wild geese
Never have such a feeling
----beautiful and sad
----circling and entangling
Full of profoundness

Light of white grass, through the quiet path
leading my easiness to look at everything
Like the leisurely floating cloud in the wild
Once more come to you closely
Even if the soul suddenly from the dissociation
Diving to the void wetland

Or like snow in the sandy road
Hearing the sound of bamboo
You the singing bird hovering over the ground
Changing my only remaining memory
Into the stars hanging from the sky
Meeting with the blurry horizon

再一次，漫步秋林，

我感到樹林在等待，

音樂在四周浮動；

如果我緊緊抓住了你，而

那悅耳的風仍在夢裡飄泊

又怎能告訴我，村裡的小河已然不同？

── 2011.9.14

── 刊登臺灣《秋水》詩刊，第 155 期，
　　2012.10

Once more, strolling in autumn forest
I feel the waiting forest
Music is floating around
If I cling to you , and
The melodious wind is still waving in my dream
How can you tell me
The village river is already different

32. 雨，落在愛河的冬夜

雨，落在愛河的冬夜
數艘白色小船上
在這多雨的港都，彩燈覆蔭下
獨自發送著溫顏

剎時，母親之河
廣大而平實
在那兒牽著勞動者的手
像從前，端視著我

啊，雨，落在愛河的冬夜
一隻夜鷺低微地呻吟
在這昏黃的岸畔，群山靜聆中
何處安置我僅存的夢？

哭吧，我以感動之淚
接受雨，和恩典
聽吧，時間的小馬上
我是永恆的騎士，覓尋黎明的歌者

32. Rain Falls in Aihe River at Winter Night

Rain, falls in Aihe River at winter night
On a few small white boats
In the rainy reason on the port
Under the shade of colorful lights
Sending out the beaming warm

Suddenly, the mother river
Broad , simple and natural
Hand in hand with the laborers
In the usual way
Gazing at me

Ah, the rain, falls on Aihe River in winter night
A night egret was moaning in the sky
On the dusky bank, mountains are listening
Where can I place my only dream

Crying, with my touched tears

I accept the rain, and the grace

Listen, the pony of time

I am the eternal knight, the singer of dawn

是的，收起遊蕩的翅膀

那生命的薔薇早已關上了門

不再憂鬱地望著我，只有躲在冷黑中的風

任遊子潤濕了瞳孔

　　── 2012.7.25 作
　　── 刊臺灣《創世紀》詩雜誌，
　　　　2012.12 冬季號，第 173 期。

Yes, draw in my vagrant wings
The rose of life has long closed her door
She no longer gazes at me, only the wind
Hidden in the black cold
Allowing the wanderer wet their pupils

33. 沒有第二個拾荒乞討婦

沒有第二個拾荒乞討婦

像她養 12 個棄嬰

過得如此辛苦，當年因無生育力

被夫家趕出門只能睡在豬圈裡

或者

漫山遍野的瘋跑準備結束脆弱的靈魂之際

如果不是村民救起

如果不是純真的幼兒給予生存的勇氣

太陽啊，你是否也毫不在意

是什麼樣的愛使這苦命女平靜下來，而她的雙手

由於要飯哺育而變得如此蒼白

而她把吃剩的地瓜絲和洋蘿蔔曬乾收好

時時提醒自己以免生病不時之需

啊，她肯定是上帝不慎遺忘的孤女

她站在那兒，瘦弱而貧疾

33. There is not a Second Beggar like Her

There is no a second beggar like her
She fostered 12 abandoned babies
She lived such a hard life
Because of her infecundity when she was young
She was driven out by her husband
And lived in the hogpen
Or
Desperately running in the wildness
When ready to finish her own life
If not saved by the villagers
If not encouraged by the pure infant
Oh, my sun, whether you are also not care
What kind of love made the miserable woman　calm down,
but her hands
So pale because of begging for feeding　her adopted
children
She stored vines of sweet potatoes and turnips
In case of her need when being ill
Oh, she must be an orphaned girl
forgotten by God
She stood there, thin and weak and poor

世界啊，快來丈量她的軀體

難道這樣的故事還不夠

讓我們一起去想想

等在社會邊緣的那些身影

難道天使之窗吝於拉開帷幕

直到那冷漠之啄敲開

夜幕從我流轉的眼神中逃離

她是否獲得了她的救贖，她的驚喜

—— 閱 2011.9.23 中國新聞網中新網一則新聞「六旬老太 19 年來收養 12 個棄嬰，靠乞討拾荒度日，但只養活了 4 個。她手上牽著大妹，背上背著二妹，筐裡挑著三妹和小妹，每天走街串巷地乞討，便是黃老太給村裡人的印象。21 歲時，因無法生育，她被夫家趕出家門，連娘家也不願意接納她。她終日渾渾噩噩地過著，一直到撿破爛時收養了棄嬰，她才有了努力活下去的希望。他們一家日子雖苦，但其樂融融。」，有感而作。
—— 2012.3.6
—— 臺灣《人間福報》副刊圖文，2012.10.01

Oh ,the world, come to measure her size

If we haven't enough stories like this

Let us to think about those

Who are waiting at the edge of the world

If angels are reluctant to open the window

Until the cold and stony pecking sounds knock

Night curtain vanishes from my moving eyesight

If she got her salvation, and her exultation

34. 當時間與地點都變了

誰在我山花牆下
用盡全身的每一個毛孔
在呼喚我？在那低密而
濃蔭的樹林中，是誰來回地走動
他用凝眸在我露臺上刻了一道痕
在潮濕的小徑上
用焦慮的雙手
呵著氣，突然攤一攤手離去
讓我匍伏的靈魂更接近天空
我百思不得其解，猜不出
那無言的字語
如今，一切都還是那樣熟悉
我看到的世界依然閃動
而你在窗外，猶如在另一個世界裡
一個古老的小屋內有一盞燈
屋外響著一個不眠的步履聲
一顆星在深秋的夜空流浪

—— 2010.12.25
—— 原載美國《新大陸》詩刊，第 123 期，2011.04
—— 轉載高雄市《新文壇》季刊，第 29 期，2012.10

34. When Time and Place Changed

Who is under my flowering wall
Trying every pore of the entire body
Calling for me? In that dense and low
Shady forest, who is walking up and down

He marks my terrace with his fixed gaze
On the humid pathway
With his anxious hands
Breathing, suddenly waves his hands and leaves
Let my pronated soul closer to the sky

I think but be puzzled, I can not guess
Those speechless words
Today, all remains the same familiar
The world I see still twinkling
Yet you're outside the window, in another world

There's a lamp in an old cabin
Sleepless footsteps echoing outside
A star wandering in the night sky of deep autumn

35. 一如白樺樹

青霧在白樺林中逃離
白樺在青霧中搖曳
小山嶺上金色花草燦然
展開在黃昏的小徑上

呵，沒有人看到我心中的懸掛
但那是它 ——
似一株嬌澀的珊瑚藤
依然逗留不去

從亙古到永遠
從怦然心動到無間距
總有一天我會放開
那個緊抓著泥土不放的身軀

—— 2010.12.23
—— 刊臺灣《海星》詩刊，第 7 期，
　　2013.03 春季號

35. Just Like the Birch

Green fog flees from the birch woods
Trees swaying in the blue mist
Golden flowers in bloom on the hill slope
Spreading over the road in the evening

Oh, no one sees my anxiety hanging in my heart
But there it is ---
Like a shy coral vine
Still lingering on

From everlasting to eternity
From the stirring beginning to the zero distance
There must be one day I 'll let go
The figure tightly clutching to the earth

36. 悼

又是八月了
雨在每一個腳印裡
都刻下一份記憶

兒啊，你到哪兒了
整整一年
難道再也聽不見祖靈的呼鳴
這歌聲曾是你熟悉的 ——
又為何遲遲不回應

只有風中抖動的白花
徐緩地
迎向我……
忽而綴成雲
忽而綴成你

又是八月了
雨啊，別再徘徊不前了
去吧，別再緊緊地緊緊地圈住我 ——

36. *Mourning*

August again
Rain carved its memory
In every step

My children, where are you
The whole year
If we hear ancestor's calling no more
The song is once familiar to you----
Why don't　you　reply

Only white flowers shivering in the wind
Slowly
Towards me
Suddenly shaping into the clouds
Suddenly shaping into you

August again
Oh, rain, do not lingering
Go away, do not tightly circling me ----

安息吧，
小林村的師生。

—— 悼小林村「八八水災」周年忌日
—— 2011.7.20 作
—— 刊美國《新大陸》詩刊，第 132 期，
　　 2012.10

May you rest in peace

Teachers and students of Xiaolin Village

—— Mourning for the death of the flood of 8th of August

37. 蘆花飛白的時候

夜幕從我流轉的眼神中逃離
我的心鋪滿憂鬱
為著我曾擁有唯一的真實
為著翱翔於星宿之間
為著許多編織的舊夢

哦，蕾貝卡，我親愛的朋友
你為什麼哭了
我可以無視我的孤獨
但無法阻止風躍回每一熟悉的名字或
注滿於流水、山丘中

世界啊，快來丈量我的軀體
為何變得如此輕靈而猶疑
每當
在清秋，萬頃原野
蘆花飛白的時候……

—— 2011.9.18
—— 刊美國《新大陸》詩刊，第 132 期，
2012.10

37. When Flowers of Reeds Flying White

Night fled from my circulating eyesight
My heart filled with depression
For the only truth I once possessed
For the soaring among the stars
For the many old dreams woven

Oh, Rebecca, my dear friend
Why are you crying
I can ignore my loneliness
But can't stop the familiar names sprung
back by the wind
Or filled in the rivers, among the mountains

Oh, the world, come to measure my body
Why does it become so buoyant and hesitate
Whenever
In cool autumn, ten thousand li of fields
When flowers of reeds are flying white……

38. 挺進吧，海上的男兒

去吧！海上的男兒
我們在你身後
看著你們無畏
波浪顛簸
無畏艦艇的驅逐
絕不在海中化作波臣
讓我感動

挺進吧！海上的男兒
白鷗為你靜默
暴風不再跟著號咷
那釣魚臺的風波依然盪漾 ──
啊，侵略者的劣徑
令我憂傷！
收復迢迢！

註：為 2012.9.25 臺灣出動史上最大的一次保釣漁船護主權行
　　動，台日艦艇曾水柱對峙，有感而作。

―― 2012.9.25 作
―― 刊登臺灣《人間福報》副刊
　　 2012.10.15 圖文

38. Push Forward, Men on the Sea

Push forward! Brave boys on the sea
We are behind you
We are saluting for your impavidity
Billowing waves driving out
Brave soldiers on the warships
Inspiring and touching to me

Push forward! Brave boys on the sea
Sea gulls are following you
Storm s are no longer howling
Waves of Fishing island still poppling
Oh, aggressors' inferior behaves
Make me feel indignation
Longing for our reoccupation

39. 漁 唱

那片金黃中有嫋嫋的歌聲。

浪似白梅有風提燈而過……

小小的島攜著不可分割的斜灣

直到彼岸，那樣地琮綠，與柔和

透射著溫情的目光 ——

而守夜的我面對

黑沉沉的星空，

像幸福的歸帆，鐘聲一樣激盪……

　　　　　　—— 2009.12.9
　　　　　　—— 刊高雄市《新文壇》季刊，第 18 期，
　　　　　　　　2010.4.1

39. Fishing Song

In the golden yellow there's singing curing up
Waves like white plum blossoms
Wind carries the lamp and passed by
A small island holds its tilted indivisible bay
To the other shore, such a jade green, and gentle
Through the warm eyesight----
Yet I ,the guard of the night facing
The deep starry sky
Like happy sails returning,
Like surging bells echoing -----

40. 停 雲

日光大道的綠
還輕吻著昨夜微雨。風
徐徐地穿過十一月堂階
看喲，這停雲。
我欣見院牆的角落裡
吟湧的辭章升向天際……
我羞澀，為了我笨拙而呆板
縱使妳
緊跟著我，在山巔，在海上
在拂曉中消失不見。
但我的伊蓮娜
這是怎樣熾烈的靈魂
搖撼了我滿被荊棘的憂傷？
哦，我聽見聲聲
木鼓來自南方，那是歌 ──
牽著我
像個母親，溫煦的目光輕輕的感歎
但願明天那伴隨在星海的淚
已經欣然在草露上徜徉。

── 2009.11.20
── 刊高雄市《新文壇》季刊，第 19 期，
2010.07

40. Halting Clouds

The green on the road of sunshine
Kisses softly the light drizzle of last night
Wind blows gently through the door of November
Oh, see the halting cloud.
I see joyfully the corner of the courtyard
Chanting the poems and rising to the sky-----

I am shy, for my clumsiness and stiffness.
Even if you
Follow me closely, on the peak, in the sea
Disappearing in the dawn
But my Elena
What kind of a blazing soul
Shaking my sorrow covered with thorns

Ah, I hear
Wooden drums from the south, which is a song---
Leading me
Like Mother, with her warm eyesight, soft sigh
Wish tears from the sea of stars tomorrow
Would change into dewdrops on the grass

41. 馬櫻丹

妳悄悄地來了
永不疲憊地
孤立一方

大地繫不住妳
遍佈的跫音
縱使踟躕於春夏秋寒

啊，那定是妳的
投影，也許是我
是我夢裡的馬櫻丹
正望著逐漸消失的亮點
恍然　霧沒

註：馬櫻丹在臺灣幾乎整年都能看到開花，可以說是個不知道疲
　　倦的植物。因枝葉含有特別的刺激氣味，所以馬櫻丹也有臭
　　草、臭金鳳等別名。

—— 2009.11.1 作
—— 刊臺灣《乾坤》詩刊，
　　2010.07 秋季號

41. Lantana

You come quietly
Never feel tired
Stand still in your place

The earth can not tie your
Spreading footsteps
Even if wavering in the seasons

Oh, it must be yours
Projection, maybe it's mine
Is lantana in my dream
Gazing at the disappearing light dot
Suddenly , lost in the fog

42. 月橘

九月，
山城的小雨
輕叩眠睡中的我
我知道黎明的使者，欣喜於
我保有的自由。

可是
雲雀呵，
你為何默默不語？
為何不坦然向我？

我可把你生命的每一天
書寫在星空中，
為你每個開花的季節
都注滿了我的溫柔……

註：月橘，又稱七裡香，是一種熱帶常青植物，帶有清香的白色
　　小花。

── 2009.11.10 作
── 刊臺灣《乾坤》詩刊，2010.07 秋季號

42. *Jasmine Orange*

September
Sprinkling in the mountain town
Clouting on me, the sound sleeper
I know the messenger of the dawn, rejoicing
In the freedom of mine

But
My dear lark
Why are you silent
Why are you not frank to me

I write every day of your life
In the starry sky
Pouring all my tenderness
Into every flowering season of you

43. 夜裡聽到礁脈

那一定源自海的發梢 ——
飄遊著，
白的夜，比它更稠密的水
顫顫地在冰天裡迴旋
湖面是一岬山影相疊，
映著斑嘴環企鵝的儀隊
在甜眠，一隻白鯊縱情
遊弋於未經探險的深礁；
我不禁循著灣邊和老樹叢
諦聽著，
這模糊中的藍灰的綠
瞳，星星也已連動；
而各處的風，滿地的葉
彷彿一起呼號
只有人類錯誤的迷失，不驚不響，
我的追尋、執著與愛的力量；
緊跟著風
許會在未來，端視海洋！

—— 2009.10.30
—— 刊美國《新大陸》詩刊，第 119 期，
　　2010.08

43. Perceiveing the Pulse of the Reef at Night

It must be from the ends of the sea's hair
Floating and wandering
White night, even dense water
Circling quiveringly in the icy sky
A shadow of a cape overlaps on the lake
Mirroring the Jackasspenguin's guard of honor
In the sound sleep, a white shark indulges
In swimming between the hidden reefs unexplored
I can not help following the bay and old grove
hearing
The blue grey of the blurry green
Look, the stars also moving
But the wind everywhere, leaves all over the ground
As if they howl together,
Only the lost of human errors,
no surprising , no sounding
My pursuing, the power of persistence and love
Following closely the wind

----maybe in the future, will be inspecting the sea

44. 三月的微風

我在小石山邊徘徊，

柿子樹攀著孤帆，

河溪雀躍向前如一簇綠光的蝴蝶。

我把一切輕浮拋入長空，

冬天的莎車歎息著

而晚鐘頻問三月雪。

註：莎車位今新疆維吾爾自治區塔里木盆地西緣。

— 2010.2.28 作
— 刊登遼寧省《淩雲詩刊》，
2010 年，第 3 期

44. Breeze in March

I strolled by the small rocky hill

Persimmon tree near the lonely sail

Stream gamboling on as green light of butterfly

I cast all the frivolous into the vast sky

Shache city in winter sighed

Evening bell knocked down the snow of March

45．秋城夜雨 —— 悼商禽

當秋雨歇在
港都夜的荒漠前
白芒花開滿山溪
行吟的雲也被擱淺
你
似一束虹光　沖向
宇宙深處
托起墜落的星辰

天使的歌音因而更嘹響

—— 2010.9.13
—— 刊高雄市《新文壇》季刊，第 21 期，
　　2011.01 春季號

45. Raining Autumn Night in the Town
— Mourning for Shang Qin

When autumn rain rests in front of
The wilderness of the night port
Meadow foams are in full blooms over the stream
The singing clouds have also been stranded
You
Like a bunch of rainbow, dashing
To the depths of the universe
Holding up the falling stars

So the songs of Angels sound even more loudly

46. 昨夜下了一場雨

你坐在開滿艾菊的岸邊

孤伶伶地佇候

也許你未曾注意

在你焦慮的目光裡，我已悄悄成長

當春天來臨

我就是那朵隱藏在飛燕草款冬裡的花

聽你神秘的詩思

在我耳畔輕聲細語

—— 2010.9.7
—— 刊高雄市《新文壇》季刊，第 21 期，
　　2011.01 春季號

46. Last Night It Rained

You were sitting by the costmary

Waiting lonely

Maybe you didn't notice

In your anxious sight, I grew up quietly

When spring comes

I am the flower hidden in the delphinium grass

Listening to your mysterious poems

And your whispers by my ears

47. 回到過去

我依稀聽到
古老
荒涼的
珊瑚群
在沿海盡端
發出呼喊
那裡是哭泣的
海百合和三葉蟲
各種小生物的故鄉

一瞬間
這世界
彷彿變了樣
在空中
在我不經意的回眸裡
那浮游的
食物鏈
因饑餓而倒下
就像失神的骨牌
對人類的嘩啦提醒

註：海百合是一種始見於石炭紀的棘皮動物，生活於海裡，具
　　多條腕足，身體呈花狀，表面有石灰質的殼。
—— 2009.11.25
—— 刊臺灣《海星》詩刊，第 2 期，2011.12 冬季號，頁 86。

47. Go Back to the Past

Dimly I hear
Ancient
Wild
Corals
At the end of the seashore
Yelling
Those are the crying
Sea lilies and trilobites
And other inchlings' hometown

Suddenly
This world
Seems changed
In the air
In my unconscious returning sight
That floating
Food chain
Crashed down because of hunger
Like glazy dominoes
Reminding human beings
The noises and clamoring

48. 水 鏡

每當我敞在湖上，
像葉脈裡的蟲，
等不及展翅 ——
哪怕夜是冬，
化蝶扇白了窗口；

每當我不想隱身，
像失聲的蟹，
不斷爬行於岸沿
直到風沒入 ——
拾起一首悲傷的歌。

—— 2011.1.21
—— 刊美國《新大陸》詩刊，第 126 期，
2011.10

48. *Water Mirror*

Whenever I row in the lake
Like a worm in the leaf vein
Hardly wait to spread my wings--- -
Even if the night is in winter
Turned into a butterfly fluttering the window white

Whenever I don't want to hide
Like a voiceless crab
Constantly crawling on the shore
Until the wind merging-----
To pick up a sad song

49. 夏至清晨

哼著山歌的稻花上
坐著一隻介蟲殼兒，戲水
飛空 —— 影子拖曳著影子
四面屏風
從跟前遛過

我擺脫了山后陰影
像綠光裡的羊
把腳步放慢
一條彎路連接無盡
水裡的雲追趕著月亮

—— 2010.3.12
—— 刊臺灣《海星》詩刊，第 5 期，
　　2012.09 秋季號

49. Summer in the Morning

Humming a folk song on the Rice flower
A cyprid sitting, playing the water
Gliding through the sky-----
shadow dragging the shadow
Wind blowing around
Passing through from me

I get rid of the shadow behind the mountain
Like a sheep in the green light
To slow down my steps
A crooked road leads to the eternity
Clouds chase the moon in water

50. 雨中的綠意

春在枝頭
雨輕盈地沾滿我的衣袖

雨呀如果你在海上
請跳到我的船兒
它是被風偷走的
我的翅膀
你可要小心輕航
用採擷來的紫丁香
朝遠遠的天邊飄去，飄去……
像一隻蝶
飛回
這夜的赭紅的溪水

我的心撥弄的詩琴
跟著徜徉在酒綠的河岸

任時間緩緩
停泊在那個雨意加深的午後
我的影子

50. The Green in the Rain

Spring on the branches
Rain drops airily wet my sleeves

Oh, my dear rain, if you are in the sea
Please jump to my boat
It's my wings
It is stolen by the wind
You should be careful
With the lilacs picked
Waving to the far away horizon
Like a butterfly
Flying back to
The ruddy brook tonight

My heart fiddles with the lute of poems
Wandering along the bank of the green river

Let time passes slowly
Anchoring in the late afternoon in rain
My shadow,

在風裡追逐
是搖晃在雲層的隴頭雲
還是落葉是鳴蟲
低微地描繪
你的微笑和眼睛

春在枝頭
雨輕盈地沾滿我的衣袖

── 2009.7.5
── 刊高雄市《新文壇》季刊，第 17 期，
　　2010.01
── 山東省《超然》詩刊，第 12 期，
　　2009.12

Chasing in the wind
Is it the heading cloud shaking
Or the fallen leaves or the chirping insects
Describing slightly
Your smile and eyes

Spring is on the branches
Rain drops airily wet my sleeves

51. 穿越

風的愁眸
懸在黑潮間
村林暗下來。點點木舟
泛著灣邊隆起的
荒涼，堆滿後灘

我穿月而來
輕彈這薄弱的時間
直到夜一同瞇起眼
不再開啓希望之弦

看靈魂如飛魚在光中潛躍 ——

—— 2009.12.31 作
—— 刊山東省作協主辦《新世紀文學選刊》，
　　2010.03

51. Passing Through

Sad eyes of the wind
Hanging between the black tides
Darkening the woods by the village
Small dots of the wooden boats
Floating with the ridgy emptiness on the bay
Wildness, stacking up on the back beach

I flew through the moon
Flicking lightly the weak time
Until the night squinting together
No longer open the chord of hope again

See the souls like flying fish diving in the light —

52. 冬的洗禮

踏出
這四面霧林
透過微光
幾株草莖
正在怯怯的萌芽

這裡的冬
沒有冷峻
只有星淚
織就成暖暖的鄉情

一切都靜止了下來
偶來幾點淡雨
鑲嵌在西窗上
似乎有意撥動滯留的時空
而多少年少不經的懵懂
竟悄然清醒如曇花的開謝

—— 2008.8.3 作
—— 刊臺灣《世界論壇報》世界詩壇，
第 143 期，第 3 版 2008.10.23

52. Baptism of Winter

Step out
The fog forest all around
Through the shimmering
Pieces of grass
Were sprouting timidly

The winter here
Has no coldness
Only has tears of stars
Woven into the warm nostalgia

Everything is still down
Occasionally a few drops of light rain
Setting in the west window
Seems like to stir up the stopped time and space
How many years of childish innocence
Quietly awake , blooming and withering
Like night-blooming cereus

53. 在靜謐花香的路上

一隻鷺，振翅了
在苗田
旋舞如縷煙

眾山動容
而桐顏沉默
它們慢條斯理地
望我

剎時
鐵道的叫賣聲
忽近忽遠

在靜謐花香的路上
一根稻草銜來一個春天
讓理念瞬間倏閃
相思成三月雪

—— 2010.12.16
—— 刊臺灣《海星》詩刊，第 3 期，
2012.03 春季號

53. On the Quiet and Fragrant Road

An aigrette, fluttering the wings
In Rice field
Dancing as a wisp of smoke

Mountains are stirred
Tung trees are silent
They look at me
Leisurely

Suddenly
Noises of peddlers from the railway
Near or far

On the quiet road with fragrant flowers
A straw bears a spring
Let the ideas flash
Longings turn into the March snow

54. 詠車城

將一路上迎面而過的防風林留在身後
我遠離大都會
以無數個形象把你幻想
在尋找飛鷹的孤途中
我獨坐黃昏
那落山風
又在隱隱作痛
箏曲般
揚一縷忠貞的清昂

註：車城 chechnya 位於臺灣屏東縣。1874 年 5 月 22 日，日軍進
　　抵石門，當地原住民據險以抗。在此役中，牡丹社酋長阿祿
　　古父子身亡。6 月 1 日起日軍分三路掃蕩原住民部落，佔領
　　後焚燒村屋並撤回射寮營地。7 月 1 日，牡丹社、高士佛社、
　　女仍社終於投降，是為牡丹社事件。

　　　　　── 2011.12.22
　　　　　── 刊登臺灣《青年日報》副刊，2012.11.17
　　　　　── 刊臺灣《新地文學》季刊，第 22 期，
　　　　　　　2012.12
　　　　　── 臺灣《乾坤》詩刊，第 65 期，
　　　　　　　2013 春季號頁 103。

54. Song for Chechnya

I stayed away from the metropolitan

Leaving behind the windbreaks along the road

Which was head-on to meet me all the way

To fancy on you with countless images

In the solitary travel of looking for eagles

I sat alone at dusk

The winter chinook winds

Aching secretly again

Like the tune of zheng

Raising up wisp of spirit of loyalty

Chechnya, the town located in Pingdong county, Taiwan province. On May 22, 1874, when Japanese invaders entered from the Rocky Gate, the local originals against the natural steepy peaks resisted the invasion bravely. In the battle, the head of the Peony tribe and his son sacrificed.

55. 山 韻

我說
我聽見了樹與星群齊舞的足音
你說
那是大雁在煙波細雨中
急急緩緩　往雲裡行

我說
我看見了千燈閃爍於萬巒峰頂
你說
那是流螢帶著清涼的鈴鐺
飛過原野　飛過沼澤　飛往自由的天庭

啊，這才想起
那杉林溪的風　施豆肥的老農
從心的隙縫
停泊在離我不遠的斜坡之地
霧還沒褪盡　蟲聲落滿胸懷

— 2011.9.2
— 刊臺灣《人間福報》副刊圖文，
　2011.10.04

55. Charm of the Mountain

I say
I heard the dancing footsteps of trees and stars
You say
These were the wild geese in the misty drizzles
Hurrying or relaxing, flying in the cloud

I say
I saw lamps glittering on the top of the mountains
You say
Those were fireflies with refreshing bells
Flying over the fields, over the cienaga
Flying to the world of freedom

Oh, I suddenly remember
The wind blowing from brook by the firs
The old farmers fertilizing the beans
From the rift of my heart
Anchoring on the slope nearby
Fog remained, chirping of insects were
full of my heard

56. 寄墾丁

第一次被大海的眼淚所觸動
是在雨後朦朧的拂曉中
不止一次
它悄悄來臨，——
用它古老而莊嚴的語調
向我問候
當那浪花用吻把記憶滌平而
你的倒影成了升騰的煙
哎，那浮雲，悠然地
在巉岩上微笑

註：據載，「墾丁」本義為「開墾的壯丁」。清領時期光緒三年
（1877 年）官方設置招墾局，募得粵籍客家人聚此搭寮墾
荒，得名為墾丁寮。十九世紀中期，因各國船隻途經鵝鑾鼻
近海，常在七星嶼附近觸礁翻覆；在美、日等國壓力下，清
廷於 1883 年建成鵝鑾鼻燈塔。中日甲午戰爭後，清軍撤離
時遂把燈塔炸毀，直至 1898 年第一次重建；但二次大戰時
又被美軍炸毀，戰後依原建築修復迄今。塔身全白，為圓柱
形，白鐵制，塔高 24.1 公尺，是臺灣光力最強的燈塔，被
稱為「東亞之光」。

— 2012.10.16 作
— 刊臺灣「國防部」《青年日報》副刊，
2012.12.16

56. For the Pioneers of Reclamation

It was in the hazy dawn after the rain

The first time I was touched by the tears of the sea

More than once

It came quietly----

In its ancient and solemn tone

Say hello to me

When waves kissing the memory smooth

Your inverted reflection was the rising smoke

Ah, the floating clouds, leisurely

Smiling on the crag

Note: The original meaning of "kending"is "the Pioneers of Reclamation". In the Qing dynasty （the 3rd year of Guangxu, 1877）, the official set up reclamation bureau to recruit hakka of Guangdong natives. They came here for building small houses which were called "kenting chambers" for reclamation. In the mid-nineteenth century, the Qing Court built the Ngoluanpi Cape Lighthouse in 1883 under the pressure from America, Japan and other countries because their vessels often overturned near the Seven star Island when going through the Ngoluanpi Cape off shore. After the Sino-Japanese war，the lighthouse was bombed out by the Qhing Army when they evacuated. It was not until 1898 the first reconstruction was done. But it was bombed out again by the US Army during the World War II. It was repaired according to the original shape after the war and has been kept in good condition so far. The lighthouse, a white cylindrical, made of galvanized iron.,24.1 feet high, is the most powerful lighthouse in Taiwan, known as "The Light of East Asia."

57. 歌飛阿里山森林

我穿過白髮的
阿里山林鐵
去尋覓童年的天真

這山泉
是個愛唱歌的小孩
音色細而堅韌
神木旁　還藏有
遊客們笑聲

當火車汽笛吶喊出
嘹亮的清音
風的裙步跟著踏響了冬林
土地的記憶
也化成一片片寧靜

我把縷縷陽光剪下

57. Songs Flying Through Forest of Ali Mountain

I go through the white haired
Forest of Ali Mountain
To search for the innocence of childhood

The mountain spring
Is a boy who loves singing
His voice fine and tensile
Beside the Divine tree, hidden
The laughter of tourists

When the train whistles
Loud and clear
Skirt of wind waves
Following the echoing of steps to winter forest
The memory of the land
Melting into pieces of tranquility

I cut down the threads of sunshine

鐫刻在櫻樹上

它竟輕輕地

輕輕地

挽住了夕陽的金鬍子

啊，還有那雲海

從何時

已網住了我每一立方的夢境

—— 2012.8.9 作　左營
—— 刊登臺灣《海星》詩刊，第 8 期，2013
　　年夏季號 —— 收錄譚五昌教授編「國際
　　漢語詩歌」，2013.11，頁 186，北京，
　　線裝書局出版。

Carve then into the cherry tree

It unexpectedly

Softly

Coiling up the gold beard of the setting sun

Oh, also that cloud sea

From when

Has netted every cubic's dream of mine

58. 旗山老街的黃昏

一條閱盡滄桑但殘存溫暖的路
一幅古樸然而不曾消逝的掛圖
一座天后宮，千萬次的護持淨土
這裡，曾是香蕉王國
這裡，曾是制糖重鎮
未來，仍是否可尋？
呵，讓我也向著前人的足音
莫要驚擾我
在浴火重生的站前
讓我與祖靈悄悄對視
像這冬陽眼中沒有一絲貪婪
像那紅燈籠長長地等待著
也許撥動旅人的夢
也許又細訴
那殿前的脊頂
雙龍拜三仙的故事

58. Dusk at Old Street of Qishan Mountain

Street witnessed long history of vicissitudes of life
But remains the feelings of warmth
A hanging picture of primitive simplicity
and never faded away
A Queen's Palace protected the pure land
millions of times
Here, it was once a kingdom of bananas
Here, it was once an old sugar town
In the future, if we can still see it here
Ah, let me also follow the predecessors
Don't disturb me
Standing before the station rebuilt from ashes
Let me quietly face the ancestors
Like the winter sun without any cupidity
Like the red lanterns waiting in a long line
Maybe stirring the dreams of the travelers
Maybe with detailed telling
The ridge in front of the palace
The story of double dragons worship three fairies
Don't call me again

莫要再喚我

我要淡然而行

輕拾那承雨牆上的淚珠

註：旗山位居高雄市中央，東毗美濃、西連田寮、南接屏東裡港
鄉、北鄰杉林。
　　該區原為西拉雅族支族馬卡道族「大傑巔社」（Taburian）
的所在地，相傳清康熙末年，住於鳳山的漳州墾民從福建汀
州招募佃人向大傑巔社人租耕土地，由於墾民在此搭建竹寮
並種植番薯，於是便有了「蕃薯藔」之稱。此地系日本殖民
統治臺灣時期的制糖重鎮，臺灣光復後是香蕉王國。
　　旗山老街以近百年歷史的旗山火車站為起點，是老街的精神
地標，沿路的小吃店頗負盛名。由於載客量驟減，旗尾線於
1978 年全面停駛，1982 年拆除所有軌道。荒廢後的火車站
曾歷經 4 次火災。老街上有指定為歷史建築的「石拱圈亭仔
腳」與仿巴羅克式街屋，此外還有重建後的旗山車站維多利
亞式的外貌及哥德式八角斜頂，與旗山區農會、天后宮等文
化資產，為全省旅遊觀光景點之一。

　　　　　── 2.12.11.16 作
　　　　　── 刊登臺灣《人間福報》副刊，
　　　　　　　2012.12.3 圖文

I want to go forward in a quiet way

Pick up the drops of tears from the wall

which stands the wind and storms for long

Note:

Qishan railway station with hundred years of history is the starting point of the town for sightseeing, and also the spiritual landmark of Qishan Old Street. Snack bars along the street are very popular. Because of the sharp decrease of the busload, the Flag tail line was fully stopped in 1978 and all the pathways were dismantled in 1982.

59. 老街吟

一紅日，浴在山枕的聚落

牽牛的故事，像透明的漏斗

順流在歷史的橫軸

我貼近街屋，米香醬油香

徐徐地 —— 徐徐地叫人不忘

我踩著無水的舊橋頭，一邊張望，一邊思想起

—— 九層粿

註：九層粿是用西螺米磨成米漿，用古法分成九層精製，層次分
　　明，其中一層還會拌入西螺醬油調味，不僅色彩美麗，Q軟
　　口感更是動人，再調配上米漿、蒜蓉醬油，十足地道臺灣口
　　味，西螺人都常把九層粿當早餐。

—— 2012.12.6
—— 刊登臺灣《海星》詩刊，第 8 期，
2013 年夏季號

59. Song of the Old Lane

The red sun, bathing in the hollow of the hill
The story of the petunia, like transparent filler
Flowing along the lateral axis of history
I come close to the house of the street
Smelling the fragrance of rice and soy sauce
Slowly, so slowly and it's hard to forget
I walk on the bridge over the dry creek
While walking I remember
—— the Nine Layered Cakes

60. 詠菊之鄉 — 開封

一、

我從新街口來
穿過龍亭公園
歷史的煙雲
遮不住秋菊的顏色

這古都城柳
輕輕繫住一隻只方舟
在風裡顛搖
在細雨的古道

走過先人路過時留下的
鐘樓、大相國寺和包公祠
那花雨的心事
也落在石階上了

只有博物館裡
顯得溫柔而蕭穆
至今仍時靜，時聞
這山長水闊的歌聲……

60. Kaifeng---Hometown of Chrysanthemums

（1）

I come from Xinjekou Street
Through the park of dragon pavilion
The Passing clouds of historical events
Can't block the color of autumn chrysanthemums

The ancient capital and the willows
Softly tie several arks
They are floating in the wind
By the ancient path in the drizzles

Walking through what left by the forefathers
Clock tower, Daxiangguo temple, Baogong hall
The worries of the flower- rain
Also falling down on the stone steps

Only in the museum
Appeared warm and solemn
Now still quiet, or sometimes we can hear
The songs of high mountains and long rivers

二、

我從鄭州裡來
穿過王屋山，直入五龍口
九裡溝的飛瀑
到底還是個幽渺地隱士

這數道城垣
像是友善地凝視著我 ——
在星空下醒著
在八荒之間吹起了笙歌
哪裡曾經是翰園碑林
哪裡曾經是汴京富麗的美景
那聲震央天的盤鼓和清明上河園
可曾激起城人的壯思逸興了

只有不朽的菊花
映照著這北方水城
至今仍時吟，時詠
遙想當年的舊事......

—— 2012.10.11 作
—— 中國河南省，開封 "全國詠菊詩歌創作
　　大賽" 獲銀牌獎〈2012.12.18 公告〉。

（2）

I come from Zhengzhou
Passing through Wangwu Mountain
Going straight into the Wulongkou Pass
The waterfalls in Jiuligou Channel
Like an mysterious and whimsical hermit

Several town walls
Seem staring at me friendly----
Being Awake under the starry sky
Blowing wind pipe for echoing far
Where the Scholars' Halls and Forest of Steles
Where was once the splendid view of Bianjing
The roaring drums
and the Qingming Riverside Landscape Park
If they could provoke the excitement and interests of the town people

Only the immortal chrysanthemums
Shines upon the Watertown of the North
We chant, we sing for them until now
For the old stories long time ago-----

61. 冬憶 ── 泰雅族祖靈祭

冬日，每一想起祖靈祭
風在流霞間悠悠地轉
在一片空曠而蒼茫的平疇上
我也向著歸巢的鷗兒
向著你的純淨　深邃張望

神啊，你是否也步履微醺
聆聽那部落長老們對吟
當熊熊的營火升起
頭目開始獻祭
溫暖了多少遊子的心

我知道你遙指發祥村而不語
而我卻只能跪下雙膝
我知道你閉上眼，在暗空
在浩漫宇宙裡為勇士舞而舒坦

61. Winter Memory — Atayal Talatuas

Winter days, when I recall Talatuas

Wind circling among the flowing clouds

On an open and vast farmland

Towards the returning gulls

I look for your purity, for your   profoundness

Oh my God, are you also taking tipsy steps

Listening to the praying of the tribal elders

When the bonfire blazing

The elders begin to pray

How many wanderers are warmed

I know, you point at the original village silently

I can only kneel down

I know you close your eyes, in the dark sky

Feeling comfort   for the Knight Dancing performed in the vast universe

Till the dawn，your hands,

直到黎明，你的雙手，像山之臂，

再次迎接苦痛的陽光⋯⋯

而我知道，那浮雲將沿著你的影子

繼續為沒有盡頭的明天

用清澈的眼睛，寂寞地回轉。

註：泰雅族的族名〈Atayal〉，原意為「真人」，或「勇敢的人」。傳說中，其祖先的起源，首先是於雪山山脈大霸尖山，其次是今南投縣仁愛鄉的發祥村（Pinsbukan），再來是位於南投縣中央山脈的白石山。後來因人口增長開始分別往西北方向、東部及西南方向分散遷移。目前，族民分佈於北部中央山脈兩側，東至宜蘭縣南澳，西至台中縣東勢，南至南投縣仁愛鄉、花蓮縣卓溪，北至烏來。其傳統舉行 Buling nutx〈靈祭祖〉的季節是小米收割後，將新谷貢獻祖靈的祭祀。因此，泰雅族的祖靈祭，也可稱為「獻穀祭」。祖靈祭舉行的時間，由頭目或長老開會商議後；晚上，要先做好蒸糯米飯（Sumul）、糯米年糕（Tnapaq-rhkil），以及糯米酒（Quaw-Tayal）等祭物。族人在天未亮、雞啼三聲時，幾乎同時抵達離部落不遠的祭場。他們手持竹棒，串刺上糕肉、水果、玉米，或用蕉葉包裹等祭物與酒，為獻給祖靈之供品，定位後就開始召喚祖靈。祭典結束的祭品向來是不帶回家的，直到天色逐漸明亮時，才開始送客。他們送客時，是用大聲的叫喊，叫著：「Usa la-usa la-」（回去吧！回去吧！）。歸途前族人須跨越火堆，以示與祖靈分隔，或象徵著污穢的潔淨，才陸續踏回部落。

—— 2012.12.13 作
—— 刊臺灣《人間福報》副刊圖文 2013.1.7
〈圖作同第一首詩〉

Like arms of the mountains
Once again come to meet
the painful sunshine-----

I know,
the flowing cloud will follow your shadow
Continue to turn lonely with their clear eyes
For the never-ending tomorrow

Note:

The tribe name "Atayal" means "genuine man" or "brave man" originally. Its traditional Buling Nutx〈靈祭祖〉is in the season when the millets are harvested. Then the tribe will contribute their new grain to their ancestral spirits. Therefore, the Atayal Buling Nutx is also known as " Grain Offering Sacrifice."

62. 冬之雪

說起北方

到底有多遠

讓你忍不住流下淚

回鄉路太長

只得把它折疊入夢

啊母親的手

從荊棘叢中向我伸來

撫摸著我苦楚的童年

　　── 2011.12.19
　　── 刊臺灣《乾坤》詩刊，第 65 期，
　　　　2013 年春季號，頁 103。
　　── 臺灣《人間福報》副刊，2013.3.26〈圖文〉

62. *Winter Snow*

When mentioning the North

How far it is

Will make me full of tears

It 's too long a way to go home

So I have to fold it into my dream

Ah, Mother's hands

Stretching from thorns to me

Touching my painful childhood

63. 我曾在漁人碼頭中競逐

我曾在漁人碼頭中競逐
那是飄雪的蠟梅氣味
啊北國！我用這裡海風傾訴
對你有多麼摯愛
到底是過去了，那閃爍的寒冷
我再不離開你視野
心中對你的想像
殷切如細弦
在你的滿林中，沒有人知道如何
或何時才能擁有泥土般堅實的愛
我癡愛的人啊搖著小風船
劃過山頭又渡滄江
你聽那不斷的猿聲，與那
映著夜幕的高塔一樣孤單
啊我的愛，那最後一瞥望見的
恰是你暖響的呼喚

—— 2012.9.30 作
—— 刊登美國《新大陸》雙月詩刊
　　第 134 期，2013.02

63. I Once Competed in the Fisherman's Wharf

I Once Competed in the Fisherman's Wharf
That is the smell of flying snow and winter plums
Ah, the Northern Land! With the wind of the sea
I expess my deep love to you
It was past anyway, the flashing cold
I will not leave your vision anymore
My heart is full of my imagination for you
As ardent as the thin strings
In your dense forest, no one knows how
Or when one can possesses
the solid love like the earth
The man I love waves a small sailboat
Acrossing the peaks and the Cang river
Please listen to the continous sound of the apes
And the loneliness as the tower against the night
Ah, my love, the last glimpse is
Just your warm calling

64. 野地

大清早
從草原上出發
鹿從林裡來
狐狸在湖邊遊蕩
水面擠滿了青蛙
那是白鷺在冰上打滑
秧雞和天鵝每天兩次
帶著青魚回家

此刻
濕地漸漸醒來
石楠和荊豆
是否還在水沼旁
千湖之陸
仍繼續保持著秘密
而有時，一個槍火
劃破靜寂 ——

獵季已開始
所有的動物都豎耳驚悸

64. *Wasteland*

Early in the morning
Setting off from the prairie
Deer out from the woods
Fox strays near the lake
Frogs crowd on the surface of the water
Aigrettes gliding on the icy lake
Corncrakes and swans twice a day
Go home with herrings

The moment
Wetland gradually awake
Moor besoms and whins
If still by the marsh
Land with thousand lakes
Still keep their secrets
Occasionally, a sound of gunfire
Breakthrough the silence------

The hunting season begins
All the animals are vigilant

在暈紅的碎石路上
肥沃的平地
映出發白的雲
和吉普車，音樂，搖滾般
向太陽方向駛去
下谷，上坡

只有我
一個孤獨的旅客
正耐心等待巴士啟動
別了，水塘
別了，野地和狗兒
在蒙著微光的蜻蜓翅芽上
一群鶴正準備遷徙遠去
牠們的身影也有絲絲落寞

　　—— 2012.9.1 為保育野地生物有感而作
　　—— 刊登臺灣《青年日報》副刊，2013.03.09

On the reddish rubble road
The fertile plain
Reflecting the pale clouds
With jeeps and music, rocking
Running towards the sun
Down the valley , up the slope

Only me
A lonely traveler
Waiting patiently for the bus to start
Farewell, the pond
Farewell, the wasteland and dogs
Above the flashing wings of the dragonfly
A group of cranes are preparing to migrate
Their backs are also lonesome

65. 白河：蓮鄉之歌

每當六月
亭台的嘻嚷笑聲不絕
那王蓮的葉盤，兀自閃爍
在微風中輕顫著
呵，白河
你是安謐的古鎮
有明鏡的水庫
流過多少人心頭
流過多少虛無的時空
在這頂山仔腳部落北側
水蓮公園頻頻點頭歡迎我
行棧道、扶疏花樹
涉蓮池、騎單車、其樂融融

白河啊，你北隔八掌溪
哺育了幾代原鄉者
你似一朵大王蓮
昂首與茫茫天空爭雄
想當年大排竹、馬稠後的聚落
先民以擔挑、推車載運

65. White River: Song of Hometown of Lotus

Whenever June comes
Laughter and frolics full of the pavilion
Trays of Jade leaves of King Lotus flashing
Waving and quivering in the breeze
Ah, White River
By the tranquil ancient town
With a reservoir of a bright mirror
You flow through people' hearts
You flowing over endless time and space
By the northern side of the tribe
At the foot of the mountain
The lotus park welcomes me
With flowers nodding their heads
Walking through the plank lane
Visiting the garden, riding bicycle, in harmony

Oh, White River
You segregate the Bazhang Brook from the north
Bringing up generations of the local people
Like a King Lotus
Raising your head to compete against the heaven
Recalling the old days
with long- row-bamboo-boats

越過白水溪畔
漸漸形成店仔口
自力更生不斷線
白河街道暖心窩
關子嶺流出黑濁泥狀的泉
枕頭山、虎頭山
山山嶺嶺唱白河

望碧雲寺寶塔呵
一草一木都問我
可知道，白河精神是什麼？
這曾是平埔族舊哆羅嘓的番地
從先人開荒地，種雜糧植甘蔗
至今豆菜面、蓮花餐
店仔口肉圓、廟口春捲
鴨肉羹…滷味均獨到
誰說那王蓮立於耀眼的水面
不是偉大的宣導者
猶如白河溪水呵流不斷
炫耀來自紅蓮朵朵
橫推水波，每當月下流螢四起
它在燈火間燦然
睡了，在這天水相間的幽靜之中

　　　　　── 2012.1.19 作
　　　　　── 刊臺灣台南文化局主辦《鹽分地帶文學》，
　　　　　　　2013.04

and the aborigines' tribes
The ancestors shouldered their baskets
pulled their carts
Crossing the bank of White River
Gradually formed the Dianzaikou Pass
Self-reliance, continue to struggle for living.
Streets along the White River prosperous
Muddy spring flows out from Guanzi Ridge
On Zhentou Mountain , on Hutou Mountain
Everywhere there are songs of White River

Looking at the pagoda in Jade Cloud Temple
Grasses and trees all ask me
 Do you know, what is the spirit of White River
Here it was once the land of Pingpu tribe.
From ancestors' exploration to plant
Growing Grains and sugarcanes
Till now beans and vegetable noodles,
lotus flower food,
Dianzaikou meatballs, Miaokou Spring rolls
Duck broth ----tastes unique .
Who can says that King Lotus ,standing over the water,
is not a great advocator
Just like the long White River,
The glory comes from the red lotus flowers
Stroking the waves, whenever fireflies fly
It will be glorious under the moonlight
Slept, in the peace between the quiet sky
and the secluded water

66. 祖靈祭

我不知道為什麼
在族人齊聚的祭場
當春石音叮咚地響
那應和的竹筒聲
也緊貼著我的耳畔
讓我歡愉又感傷

啊，美麗的拉魯島
在自由中騰飛
森林與山也跟著我歌唱
那痛苦的精靈
已不再抖顫
原來臼與杵
可以是這樣融合
原來生 老 病 死
也是一種本然

66. *Talatuas*

I don't know why

In the offering field where clansmen gathered

When the grinding stone tinkled

The echoing sound of bamboo tubes

Also close to my ears

Let me feel both joyful and sorrowful

Ah, beautiful Lalu Island

Rise in the free sky

Forests and mountains sing together with me.

The suffering spirits

No longer tremble.

So, the mortar and pestle

Originally inosculate closely

So the death and life

Also a nature

我不知道為什麼

像只孤鷹，惆悵而迷惘

那記憶裡的魚姬傳說

已攫走了我的靈魂

把我輕輕地帶過泛紅的潭水

回到溫存的夢鄉

註：邵族（Ita Thao），聚居於南投日月潭一帶；為臺灣族群人
數最少的原住民族。每年為迎接新年來到，邵族人齊聚杵音
祭場舉行祖靈祭。每戶族人帶著祖靈籃 ulalaluwan〈通稱為
公媽籃〉置放祭場，再由先生媽（女祭司）吟唱傳統歌謠祈
福。儀式完成後，各家將祖靈籃帶回祭拜，而祖靈祭期間，
族人要先獻一缸酒給先生媽作為儀禮，並從初一至初三，挨
家挨戶喝酒，稱為 tuktuk，意即「飲公酒」。祖靈籃內盛祖
先遺留下來的衣飾，以代表祖靈之存在公媽籃內。凡是族中
之重要祭儀，諸如播種祭、狩獵祭、拜鰻祭、豐年祭等，都
以公媽籃為供奉的對象，族人備酒、飯、糕等為獻品。這種
敬祀祖靈的方式，是邵族得以成為族群中獨立一族的最主要
特徵。而如何繼續維護邵族人的生活、語言、文化的風貌，
實值得政府部門重視。

— 2013.1.24 作
— 刊臺灣《青年日報》副刊，
2013.04.04

I don't know why

Like a solitary eagle, melancholy and lost

The legend of　LadyYuji in my memory,

Has taken away my soul

Bring me gently through the reddish pool

back to my warm hometown

67. 墨菊

你是多年前

從菊譜裡　飛出的

草龍

時間的長河中　笑容依是

如此嫻靜

而我

只是路過時　不慎回首的

行者　只想將你

匯入飄遊的夢中

—— 2013.1.8 作

—— 刊臺灣《笠詩刊》，第 294 期，
　　2013.04

67. Black Chrysanthemum

You are the grass dragon

Flying from the chrysanthemums

Many years ago

In the long river of time, smiling still

So quiet

But me

A passersby, by chance look back

Only want to keep you

Into my wandering dream

68. 春芽

夜窗外

醉不勝吟的月

攬住了我

齊看

大地是否

樹綠交加

花滿春和

　　—— 2013.1.7
　　—— 刊臺灣《笠詩刊》，第 294 期，2013.04
　　—— 刊山東《春芽兒童文學》創刊號，
　　　　第一期，2013.06

68. Spring Buds

Outside the night window

Intoxicated moon

Hugged me

Let's see it together

If the earth

With trees green

If flowers are fragrant

In the spring garden

69. 一個雨幕的清晨

一個雨幕的清晨
簷滴
輕巧地溜過 沉默的街燈
我想起了既往，痛悼早逝的靈魂
在空曠中，雀聲急急去向某地
外界彷彿已經風止雨停

我守持著寂寞
生怕雨水將我的記憶微微打濕
生怕風兒也找不到它的斑痕
生怕斷片的祈禱
在心靈深處
被大火鑄成一片荒蕪

又是六月
回想你過去眼神的時辰

69. An Early Morning in Rain

Morning with rain curtain

Eaves drops

Lightly slipped through, silent street lamps

I thought of the past, grieved over the early passed

In the open, birdsongs hurried to somewhere

Outside it seemed already in peace without storms

I kept my loneliness

In case raindrops would wet my memory

And the wind would not find its cicatrices

For fear of the prayer of fragments

In the depths of my soul

Be burned into the barren

It's June again

Recalling your eyesight in the past

從廣場席捲而來

重重地叩擊的聲音

我在風中搖晃時間

時間像窗外迷路的蜥蜴

倦怠地凝望著我

等待烏雲輕鬆地穿過

緩緩踱步的黃昏

—— 2013.3.1

—— 刊臺灣《笠詩刊》，第 294 期，2013.04

—— 收錄中國《北都文藝》主編
《2013 年中國及海外漢詩選》

It swept across the square

With the heavy knocking sound

I was shaking the time in the wind

Time like the lost lizard outside the window

Staring at me wearily

Waiting for the dark clouds passing breezily

And the slowly pacing twilight

70. 夏日長風

當森林的小溪
遇上驟雨湍急
紛紛
爭著逃向大海
停在地平線上
自熙攘直至寬廣
只見　太陽兀自靜定
流影如銀沙

又是奔騰的一夏
讓我聆聽於浪濤
如激昂的嘯歌
把煩瑣擲向水舞
把豪情揮灑蒼穹
我是挺直的小草
綿延萬里的南風

—— 2008.8.10 作
—— 刊臺灣《乾坤》詩刊，第 50 期，
2009 年夏季號

70. Sweeping Wind in Summer

When the creeks in the forest
Come across the rushing showers
One after another
They race to the sea
Ceasing at the horizon
Rushing from bustling to the vast
Only see, the sun holds on calmly
Swaying shadow like Silver sand

Another galloping summer
let me listen to the billowing
Like boiling whistles
Throw the troubles to the dancing water
Spread the Grand ambitions to the sky
I 'm an upright grass
I'.m the long south wind
Stretching thousands of miles

71. 江岸暮色

滿枝杏葉的樹叢

像是空山的彩蝶

緩緩飛來

靜聽

松濤

在依依的薄染

層巒疊翠的雲霞

更有幾點歸雁

悲鳴

滿霜風

月寒前

夕陽

送潮在

天之一角與隔岸的傳鐘

　　　——2009.1.9 作
　　　——刊登新疆《綠風》詩刊，2009.03
　　　——臺灣《乾坤》詩刊，第 50 期，
　　　　　2009 年夏季號
　　　——泰國《中華日報》，2009.08.11

71. Dusk by the River Bank

Apricot trees thick with leaves

Like colorful butterflies in the sky

Flying softly

Quietly listen

The waves of Pine trees

In thin fog

layers of jade clouds

A few wild geese return

Lamenting

Full of frost and wind

Under the cold moon

Setting sun

Moving tides

One corner of the world

Echoing of the bells from the other bank

72. 老　街

在暮靄裡簇擁暗喊著

有力的宣言

我拍下鏡頭

鏡頭隱在百年不曾改變的

畫面

無法看穿的陰影下

那錯落的叫賣聲　勾劃出

一張張親切的臉

── 2009.01.02 作

── 刊臺灣《世界論壇報》，第 157 期，
2009.03.05

72. Old Street

Dense evening mist , silent crying

A powerful statement

I took the photo

Hidden the unchangeable for a hundred years

The picture

Under the shadow you cannot see through

That echoing of the peddlers , outlining

Amiable faces

73. 夢土的小溪

在我的回首中，落梅遲遲，更覺相留
別是春歸遠去的時候
妳是無人的綠原的一粒花果
因為波光而不期然的淹入了下游 —— 也許
妳堅持。那是唯一的選擇
妳同在風中吟唱
風在碎石子的小路上徒步著
這裡有的是遠山凝寂
時而彌望，時而歡容
直到有一個相當模糊
渺渺小小的回音，仍然掙扎著
默喚了我
而夜裡的白樺，也使盡全力
向上等候

—— 2009.01.14 作
—— 刊臺灣《葡萄園》詩刊，第 183 期，
　　2009 年秋季號

73. Brook in the Dreamland

In my memory, plums falling late

Even more reluctant to leave

Parting when spring is gone

You are a grain of fruit in the wild greenland

With the light of the waves flowing to the downstream- maybe

You persist. That's your only choice

You sing songs in the wind

And wind is on the gravel road

Plenty of distant mountains and silent views

Sometimes watching, sometimes joyous

Till one rather blurring-----

Tiny echoing, still struggling

Silently awaking me

And birches in the night, also make efforts

Up towards and waiting

74. 一方小草

小煤屑路
慢慢兒的
從山嘴裡穿
一棵棵
不知名的
樹
幽幽地庇護我
我底眼睛
竟瞬間
漾成水雲
無力的
牽著夕陽直入古藤叢中
驀然發現，隱在暮煙
一片一片……的小草，也攀上山坡
一如真正的行者
在星輝底下
彎了腰也挺得
灑脫自在

—— 2009.01.30 作
—— 刊美國《新大陸》詩刊，第 111 期，
　　2009.03

74. Grass in one Corner

A narrow cinder footpath
Slowly
Through the mountain ridge
One by one
Nameless
Trees
Sheltering me silently

My eye sight
Suddenly
Flowing like clouds and water
Faintly
Pulling the setting sun into the old vines

At this moment, hidden in the evening smoke
Pieces of ... grass, also climbing up the hill
Like a real traveler
Under the shining stars
Even with bended waist also stand straight
Free and easy

75. 霧裡的沙洲

浮著淺淺的水面
洗盡新生的地
像是滴漏的雲，流過曾文溪口北岸
在我守著候鳥最期待指向的經緯
忽而聽到遠方的訊息
彷彿秋晴背著我隔海相望

當我離去，古風依依
你一一採集我底足印如細浪
當我回首，你是我載不動的愁
停靠在蘆花深處，與風切的暮色
而幾滴清露喚起的
千萬端緒卻悄悄在淡月裡
飄來盪去……

—— 2009.02.05 作
—— 刊登河北省《新詩大觀》第 55 期，
　　2009.04，頁 12。

75. The Alluvion in the Fog

Shallow water
Washing the newborn land clean
Like clouds from the sandglass
Flowing through north shore of Zengwen Estuary
When I abide with the migrant birds
with eager expectation for the altazimuth
Suddenly the message comes from far away
As if cool autumn carries me across the sea

When I leave, the ancient wind breeze still
You---- gather ripples from my footprints
When I look back,you are the sorrow I can't bear
Deep down among reeds and windy twilight
The troubled feelings aroused by drops of dew
were flapping about
All among the faint moonlight ……

76. 春 天

天光之前
泥土已經甦醒
之後，它走訪了許多視窗

梭巡綠野時
它輕喚了蠶蛹
俯視羊群時
它點醒了牧童
經過避雨的人
它揮灑了彩虹

而今，風箏依然
盤旋我的青空
我呆呆地望著
它竟然邀我舞動

── 2008.6.14
── 刊登河北省《新詩大觀》，第 54 期，
　　2009.02

76. Spring

Daybreak
Awaking the land
Then ,she called on many windows

When passing and painting green the wild
She awoke the pupas
When overlooking the sheep
She roused the shepherds
When passed by the men sheltering the rain
She sprayed the rainbow

Now, the kite is flying
Hovering over my head
I am staring into the sky
She is inviting me to dance

77. 黃昏雨

雨高懸在殿前
佔據著山頭
連綿到河岸匍匐在
綠蔭下，突然消失於下墜的夕陽中

因為來去匆匆
它的身影有鑲邊玻璃那麼亮
小時候我就是鏡裡的雪河
披上暈紅的新裝，等待花落

這場雨把院落靜得恍如出世
也帶來最驚喜的聲音
卻老聽見
自己的腳步踏在
石板面上的
回聲

—— 2008.09.05 作
—— 刊河北省《新詩大觀》，第 54 期，
　　 2009.02，頁 16。

77. Rain at Dusk

Rain curtain is hanging high in front of the palace
Occupying the mountain top
Stretching to the river bank, creeping
Under the green shade
Suddenly disappears in the setting sun

Coming and leaving in a hurry
Its figure, bright as a trimmed glass
When young, I was a snowy river in the mirror
Covered with new rosy clothes
waiting for the flowers falling

The rain silences the yard like a wonderland
Also brings the most pleasant surprising voice
But always hear
My own footsteps
On the slab stones
Echoing

78. 大貝湖畔

一棵濕綠的樹
輕彈著鐘琴
湖面
靜謐地
前來傾聽

直到曙光
擦白了葉影
晨霧似白貓的足音
我跟著亮點走

當帶路的星子隱退
我的猶豫
都將涼醒

—— 2008.11.02 作
—— 刊登河北省《新詩大觀》，第 54 期，
　　2009.02，頁 16-17。

78. Bank of the Dabei Lake

One wet and green tree
Gently playing the glockenspiel
The lake
Silently
Come round listening

Until the dawn
Whitening the shade of leaves
Morning mist, like footsteps of a white cat
I follow the light spots

When the leading stars fade
My hesitation
Would be cold to wake up

79. 木棉花道

一盞盞
亭亭的金燈
倒映和逐流於
石橋的兩側

花萼被調和
如三月黃昏的嬌羞
赴遠到雲團裡
貼近那望不盡的茂林 ——
而遠處土皁上的炊煙
順著一彎清淺
牽出山中之月
於是寺院的紅磚道上
忘不了的，是那綿密的
輕愁

　　　　— 2009.02.06 作
　　　　— 刊登臺灣《葡萄園》詩刊，第 182 期，
　　　　　2009 年夏季號

79. Path of Kapok Flowers

One by one
Line of golden lights
Reflected and flowed
Along both sides of the stone bridge

Calyxes are dyed
Into shy color of the dusk of March
Spreading into the clouds afar
Closing uo to the never-failing dense forest----
Smoke of kitchen chimneys from distant mounds
Following a clear and shallow river
Leading along the moon from the hill
Then on the red bricks of the temple lane
The unforgettable, is the endless
Slight melancholy

80. 走在彎曲的小徑

沒有生氣的
給他一雙高翔的振翅
沒有甦醒的
給他一顆燃起的雄心

我有意氣
也有豪情
前面，已沒有多餘的視線
只有無休無止的馳騁

在沒有妳燦爛如夏的日子裡
我是個擦身而過的
行者，正待回頭轉身
開創命運

—— 2009.02.08 作
—— 刊臺灣《世界論壇報》，第 153 期，
　　2009.04.09

80. Walking on the Winding Path

To the lifeless

Give him a pair of frying wings

To the slept

Give him a heart of burning ambition

I am spirited

I have ambition

ahead, there is no excrescent sight

Only the endless galloping.

In the days without your splendid summer

I am the passing

Travler, ready to turn back

Creating my way of destiny

81. 驀然回首

我努力捕捉
那守在雲堆裡的陽光如流星的眼波

白鳥齊飛，空餘的笑聲低回
在我感動的一刻
山盡的茅屋又多了份凝重，那是
這一地金黃自雨後沖刷的青石階上
只聞微風向甜美的小草殷勤問候

前路一直延伸著
而我已別無所求
只要拐個彎
就會看見栩栩如生的楓紅

── 2009.02.23 作
── 刊臺灣《葡萄園》詩刊，第 182 期，
2009 夏季號

81. Suddenly I Turn Around

I try to catch

waves of eyesight like sunshine

From the meteor defending by the clouds

White birds flying, laughters echoing low

In that moment I was moved

The hut in the end of the mountain

is more dignified, that is

The gold yellow on the stairs of the blue stone washed clean by the rain

Hearing the breeze's greetings to the sweet grass

The road is stretching forward

And I have no more demands

As long as I take a turn

I shall see the vivid red maples

82. 岩川之夜

野溪
是密林琅琅的樂音

圈圈螢光
披雪守在飛瀑外
一路緊緊相連

黃金雨季不來

而等待
變成阿勃勒花海
來送還它的思念

　　　—— 2009.5.5 作
　　　—— 刊臺灣《葡萄園》詩刊，第 183 期，
　　　　　2009 年秋季號

82. Night by the Rocky River

Wild creek
Is the music of the dense forest

Circles of the fluorescence
Covered with snow outside the waterfall
Connected closely all the way

Precious rain season does not come

Yet waiting
Becomes Golden shower of flowers
To return back its longing

83. 河階的霧晨

銅門村外
階崖下
奔騰著
溪底激盪　的洄瀾

風浪上
一畦畦
茶園
雲飛在鶴岡

沿徑而行
這一次回來
只因奇萊北峰
相繼彩排
你原有的顏色

我也不過是
沖淡潭畔
匆匆而又
頻頻回首的過客

註：1.西班牙文「波瀾」、「海浪」之意,與「洄瀾」有同義之趣。
　　2.奇萊北峰位於臺灣花蓮縣，海拔標高 3607 公尺，隸屬太魯閣國家
　　　公園管轄。
　　　　　—— 2009.6.9 作
　　　　　—— 刊美國《新大陸》詩刊，第 113 期， 2009.08

83. Misty Morning by the River Terrace

Outside Tongmen village
Under the cliff
Galloping
Clean ripples at the bottom of the stream.

On the waves
Farmland
Tea garden
Flying clouds over the Crane Hill

Walking along the path
This time coming back
For the North Peak of Shilai
Rehearsal successively
Your original color

I am only but
Wading through the streams
In a hurry
One traveller frequently looking back

84. 一滴寒星

浪鼓
花林中
總是忽起忽落

江面的楓葉
一樣素潔
只有我傾跌進深谷
隨風帆
凌波而來

一隻山鷸
響透這暗綠的夜
緊依空枝
交結著我的飄零

在　望不盡的
海岸之前
輕輕地
輕輕地緩下腳步
如果妳側耳聽

84. A Drop of Cold Star

The wave drum
Among flowery woods
Rising up and down

Maple leaves floating on river
Plain and clean
Onlyme fall into the deep valley
Following the sail
Rising on the waves

A partridge
Chirping through the dark green nigh
Resting on the bald branches
Melting into my solitude

On the boundless
Seabeach
Gently
Gently softening my steps
If you listen carefully

與其劃破時空而熱烈輝耀
不如一掠而過
只看見向前的我

── 2009.07.07 作
── 刊美國《新大陸》詩刊，第 113 期，
　　2009.08

It's better to pass through swiftly
Only seeing my marching forward
Than to be brilliant and glittering
Breaking the time and space

85. 夢裡的山谷

秋田無雨
雲棲在林外的桑麻野道
直到霧氣彌漫
將天地融於地平線
後方是近乎單色的島嶼
稀疏地飄起幾縷青煙

秋田無雨
雲凝視古老歷史的碎片
聚落的
浮
沉
一棵棵橄仔樹
依稀可辨
而後星子互偎環伺著曠野
日夜輪替

85. Valley in the Dream

Autumn field has no rain

Clouds hovering over forest by the wildness

Until the foggy mist is filled

Melting the skyline and horizon

Backside the dull colored islands

Sparcely scattered floating smoke

Autumn field has no rain

Coulds stared at the shattered history.

Gathering

Rising

Falling

Olive trees

Barely recognized

Then stars snuggled up to the wild

Days and nights are in turn

還可聽到荊棘的聲音

是飛鳥的長鳴？

月光在森林狩獵

秋田無雨

—— 2009.06.06 作
—— 刊臺灣《葡萄園》詩刊，第 184 期，
　　2009 年冬季號
—— 山東省《超然詩刊》，第 12 期，2009.12
—— 菲律賓馬尼拉版《世界日報》副刊，
　　2009.08.06
—— 美國《新大陸》詩刊，第 116 期，2010.02

Also hearing the whispers of the thorn bush

Is this the long chirping of the flying birds

Moonlight is hunting in the forest

The rainless autumn field

86. 野渡

一隻鷹　擎起
懸崖邊的天空
點點水鳥　化成
細浪漂漂　流入
相連的大地
慢慢飄散
不知道是什麼生存的希望
鼓動著你
遠渡楳子溪口
夕陽下，但
你杳逝的背影
顯得如此孤傲
就這樣
避開了
風雨　驚濤
緊跟著紅太陽
你似乎即將沒入灰藍的遠方
卻又像是要停泊在我的心上

—— 2009.7.22 作
—— 刊美國《新大陸》詩刊，第114期，2009.10

86. *Wild Ferry.*

An eagle, holding up
The sky by the cliff
Dots of seagulls, melting
Tiny waves , flowing
The stretching land
Slowly scattering

What is the hope for existence
Encourage you
Drive you
To the far away Piaozi Pass
Under the setting sun,but
The figure of your fading back
Lonely and proud

Hence
Away from
Wind and rain, billowing waves
Followed the glowing sun
You seem to merge into the grayish blue far way
But also seem to reside inside my heart

87. 春深

藍灰色的煙波，是慌亂
的羊群。夜逃出森林
尋找豐饒女神，
飛鳥粉妝水鏡。

此刻，雨雲中，
晨曦凝成帶裳
的明湖，雞唱，聲聲
似草碧的春紅。

春在柳梢，
杜鵑輕啼尚早，
所有青山白水、開始暗移
瀟瀟的腳步；

一笛風聲，
將漫飄的客夢
點醒，隱忍，

87. Deep Spring

Blue gray smoke, panic
Sheep flock, the night flies out of the forest
Looking for
The fertile goddess
Flying birds and pink water mirror

This moment, in the rainy clouds
The dawn curdled into veiled
Clean lake, the cock sings, songs
Like the red and green of the spring

The spring in on the tip of the willow
Cuckoo sings still too early
All the green mountains and white water
Began to move quietly
With the whistling footsteps

A flute of wind
Making the floating dream of the travler
Awake, tolerateding

一切在空無、沉潛、寄吟。

回首歸程，綠已深，
這日線的紅影有多長？
怕是獨我幽存的情更深，
啊，半籠的江景。

—— 2009.7.8 作
—— 刊臺灣《新文壇》季刊，第 16 期，2009.10
—— 山東省《超然詩刊》，第 13 期，2010.06

All is empty, sinking, sighing

Looking back for the journey
The green has been deep
How long is the threads of the red shadow
I'm afraid only my thinking is deeper and lonely
Oh, the hazy river view

88. 在積雪最深的時候

漸漸掩埋了
公路和我
風不想停歇
啄那細枝號鳴的心事
夜沉默了
鷓鴣孤鳴
我站在叉道前
等待樹叢冰柱的脆聲
夜墊著腳尖
一一採擷
悲傷的足印
一隻害羞的鼴鼠
瞄著我及我的夢境
噢，這冗長的冬季
你睡著了嗎
不，其實我是不在乎的

—— 2010.9.30
—— 刊臺灣《乾坤》詩刊，第 64 期，
　　2012.11 冬季號

88. *When the Snow is Deepest*

Buried bit by bit
The highway and me
The wind is reluctant to stop
Pecking on the agony tied to the twigs
The night is silent
A lonely partridge chirping
I'm standing in front of the crossroad
Waiting for the crisp sound from the icicles
Night tiptoed approaching
------plucking

Sad footprints
A shy flying squirrel
Aiming at me and my dreamland
Oh, the long winter days
Are you still sleeping
Oh no,I actuallydon't care

89. 米仔麩

米仔麩是鏡頭下一張泛黃的照片
我瞇著老花眼
透過方形的光束，去撿拾當年
落滿一地的笑靨
冬夜喝上一碗
猶如走過一條狹長的小巷
門前的春聯
長凳底身影
啊，我見到了蒼白的父親
以緩慢的語調
以慈悲的眼神
喚著我回家的聲音 ——
然後
空氣中
飄浮著那種
熱呼呼的氣味……

—— 2008.8.27 作
—— 刊重慶市《中國微型詩》，總第 18 期，
2009.06

89. Rice Bran

Rice bran is a yellowish photo under the lens

I narrow my presbyopic eyes

Through the square beam, to pick up the year that

Covered with dimpled smiles everywhere

Drink a bowl of wine in the winter night

As if going through along a narrow alley

Spring scrolls in front of the door

Shadows of the benches

Ah, I see my pale father

With a slow voice

With kindness in his eyes

Calling me to go home-----

Then

In the air

Floating the warm smell......

90. 魯凱族「黑米祭」

啊，倘若我的夢飛向
部落與尚未遺忘的歌聲懷抱
擺脫都會的煩囂
重聽那黑米謝神的故事
倘若我釋放的靈魂嬉遊
穿越紫斑蝶的河谷
那麼，我將與族人圍舞
那麼，我將感恩並分享
喜悅，尊嚴和榮耀
但曠原對我反復呼喊
日子也彷彿回到最初
而所有湧現的淚和
相聚的歡笑與離愁
也終將熄於那遠路盡處
淡藍的夜霧中。

90. Rukai Tribe's "Black Rice Fete"

Ah, if only my dream flies

To the tribes and embraces with the songs

which have not been forgotten

I will get rid of the hustle and bustle

Listen to the story of black rice again.

If only my free soul would wander

Passing through the valley of purple butterflies Then,

I would dance with the clansmen

Then, I would be grateful and share

The joy, dignity and the glory

Yet the vast land calls me repeatedly

The days seem to return to the original

All the tears came forth and

Laughters of gathering, sadness of leaving

May extinguished into the light blue fog

at the end of the remote night road

註：魯凱族主要分佈在高雄縣茂林鄉、屏東縣霧台鄉及台東縣東興村等地。其中，茂林鄉多納部落獨有的「黑米祭」，在每年 11 月秋收後舉行勇士舞、盪秋千、搗黑米等活動。而 傳說中黑小米的故事，源於一位多納婦女因農忙而將孩子放在水潭邊，以聽見哇哇哭聲來辨別孩子的安全。但某日卻無聽見哭聲，這焦急的母親在一次夢中，聽見水神告訴她不忍孩子一直哭泣，將他帶走並代為扶養直到長大，但希望部落能種植黑米謝神。

（不在這裡：知本位於台東市西南郊 17 公里處，因溫泉及森林遊樂區等自然景觀而盛名。區內原住民計有卑南族、魯凱族、排灣族等族群。

3. TISAU「曲冰」部落是南投縣仁愛鄉萬豐村的舊名，是臺灣布農族分佈最北的一支，全村數百居民；因濱臨中央山脈，正處於臺灣地理的中心位置，亦是臺灣之心。曲冰之名始於 1981 年挖掘到的史前聚落遺址「曲冰遺址」；1988 年間，曲冰遺址被列為三級古跡。部落位居於濁水溪上游，沿岸一度農田密集，居民多以務農為生。除了曲冰橋，部落後糯米椒田叉路上山，有聖母亭、十字山。此外，還有多條生態步道、原始林、精靈瀑布、天使瀑布群、曲冰峽谷等，是香糯米故鄉。

— 2013.4.8
— 刊登臺灣《人間福報》副刊，
2013.4.30 圖文

第 252 頁〈魯凱族黑米祭〉插畫，刊《人間福報》2013.4.30

第 300 頁〈月桃記憶〉插畫，刊《人間福報》2013.7.2

91. 母親 (一)

那雙長繭的手
與揮不盡的汗水
還有那聲音
有時像花蝶飛出牆前
在心中閃爍
有時像雨絲飄忽
如期而至。

多少次？在風中閃現
彷彿月落星移……
然而她專注而笨拙地
抄寫經書，來自寧靜
那熟悉的眼眸
在夢底深處
我慌亂地將她喊出。

—— 2013.5.8

—— 刊登臺灣《人間福報》副刊，2013.5.28.圖文

91. Mother 1

Her calloused hands
Her nerver-ending sweat
And her voice
Sometimes like the colorful butterflies
flying out of the wall
Twinkling in my heart
Sometimes like the drizzling
Coming as I expected

How many times?　Flashing in the wind
As if the moving of the moon and stars-----
Yet she was concentrated and awkward
Copying the scriptures, calmly
Her familiar eyes
In my deep dream
I shout out for her confusedly

92. 母親 (二)

童年雖然貧困，
挨著老屋中的一角
有個影子坐在昏燈下，
那雙長繭的手，在微明中，若隱若現，
一把陳舊的椅，
針線用舊了反而安慰。
空氣中有著鮮潔的肥皂香
如此熟悉如月明 —— 噢，母親。

我愛，那髮上每一處泛白的花朵
與每一個偶現的歡顏
就像蝴蝶在風之上飛舞；
而妳是偉大深根的女使，
雖則故鄉那莿桐花和綠野
正把小小的我藏在群星之間，而我
總是想尋妳的影子也不太可得
噢，母親 ——

92. Mother 2

Poor childhood
By the corner of our old house
Her shadow under the dim light
A pare of hands with callus
In the owllight, half concealed
A worn chair
Needles and threads used for a long time
With comforting sense
Refreshing fragrance of soap in the air
So familiar like the moonlight
Oh , my Mother

I love,every blossom of her grey hair
And occasionally appeared soothing smiles
Like butterflies flying in the breeze
Mother, the great angel of the earth
Though I ,the tiny one ,
was concealed among the stars
By the Citung flowers and green wildness
I always try to find your silhouette
Oh, Mother ---

多少次？在風中閃現

月臺離別來回不停揮動的手

提水洗衣或耕田 ——

或那舊衣衫的。我目擊無數次

抄寫經書的手，已屆滿二十年

那無怨尤的眼眸，在夢底深處

我慌亂地將她喊出

噢，母親 ——

—— 2014.7.11 作
—— 獲第六屆「漂母杯」文學獎第二等獎於 2014.7 頒獎於淮安市，收入臺北聯經出版《母愛，愛母》2014.10 出版，頁 151-152。

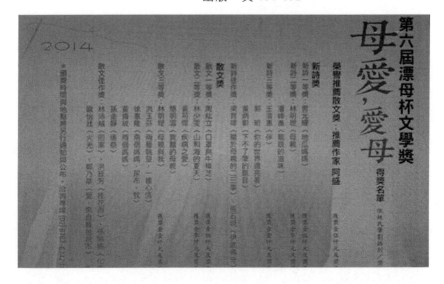

How many times, flashing in the wind
Your hands for farewell waving at platform
Fetching water, washing
and furrowing in the field----
And your worn clothes
How many times I see
Your copying of Buddhist sutra
for twenty years
Your eyesight calm
In my deep dream I bursted out my calling
Oh , Mother-----

93. 山寺前一隅

啊，但願此刻在山寺，趁這冬夜
我從夢中甦醒，猶記得去年
五葉松前，落霞滿天
聽，那歌雀
在院牆，在月的眉睫

啊，隆冬一過，三月翩至
綠芽鑽出頭兒，蜜蜂前來探尋
聽，那誦聲
映照著枝條下的草地
元宵燈火閃晃，如此神聖

究竟是為了什麼？
難道只想捕捉一次永恆

93. One Coign in Front of Mountain Temple

Ah, I wish I were in the mountain temple now
While it is the winter night
I wake up from my dream, still remember last year
In front of the Pine Trees
The sky covered with the rosy clouds
Listen, the singing birds
On the walls, on the moon's eyebrow

Ah,when winter passes , March comes
Green buds shooting out, bees arriving
Listen, the reading sound
Reflecting the lawn under the branches
Lanterns of festival twinkle with sacred light

Anyway
Is it for one capture of eternity

我猜了又猜啊，原來那

生命的荒漠，已得到泉湧的安寧

—— 2013.2.24

—— 刊中國澳門《華文百花》2013.01，
　　總第 18 期，2013.08

I try to guess
Oh, it turns out
The desert of life,
has reached the peace of the spring

94. 回鄉 (一)

我，流浪者，來這裡租地耕作
可是這裡卻不見故鄉的煙霧與泥土
也看不到故鄉的鷹
那些被毀壞的橋，經歷多次風災的路
那些頹垣茶村，啊，哪裡有我立身之處？
你看那雲豹故鄉，有祖先的足印
過去我種小米和香蕉
也種茶葉和樹豆
如今只剩下回憶
那些祭祀慶典和吃過的山肴

回鄉，是我唯一的出路
回鄉，是我唯一的渴求
只有湖神依然為我祝福
將我的歌，藏進
他深而悲傷的眼眸

註：在部落論壇中，多位專家提及，好茶、瑪家、長治、霧台鄉
　　等族人，都希望政府重視讓他們回鄉耕種的意願，避免重建
　　政策淪為族民心中的痛。

　　—— 2012.12.26 作
　　—— 刊臺灣《笠》詩刊，第 295 期，2013 年 6 月。

94. Back Home 1

I, one vagrant, coming to cultivate the leased land
But there is no the smog and earth of homeland here
And there is no trail of eagles of homeland too
Bridges destroyed, roads undergone wind disasters
Ruins of tea villages,
oh, where should I settled down

You see the hometown of leopards
where footprints of ancestors left
I used to grow millets and bananas
Also tea and pigeon peas
Today only the memory left
About the worship ceremonies and food eaten

Go home, it's my only way out
Go home,it's my only desire
Only the God of the lake blesses me
Hidden my songs into
His deep and sorrowful eyes

95. 回鄉 (二)

我六月的夜晚
上故鄉普悠瑪的岸
消失的溪橋和田野是灰色的
月光仍憂傷。

流浪的風啊
賣力跟著我爬上崗
一行淚珠
沿著臉龐向群山呼喊。

我唯一要說的
三小時三十分鐘長
四十年等待的
翹盼。

啊 —— 歲月悠悠，我
知道，彼岸的凱旋門
有領唱老調的耆老和
酒香。

95.Return Back to My Homeland

At the night of June
I walked on the bank of Puyuma River
The grey is the disappeared bridge over the brook and field
And the moonlight is still gloomy

Oh, the wandering wind
Following me desperately to the hillock
A line of teardrops
Along the cheeks to shout to the mountains

The only thing I want to say is
Three hours and thirty minutes long
Forty year's
Yearning

Oh----leisurely passing time, I
Know, the arch of triumph on the other shore
There is the senior leading the old tunes and
The fragrance of Wine

啊 —— 多麼崇高而奇妙
Puyuma —— 我永久的愛
你聽得見嗎？在每一站
我哼唱的 —— 歌聲如鵲鳥。

註：Puyuma，普悠瑪號，其名源自卑南族部落大首領所在地「普
　　悠瑪」，亦有「集合團結」的意思；同時這也是卑南鄉以及
　　臺東市南王部落的稱呼。

　　　　　　　　—— 寫於 2014.7.1 臺東
　　　　　　　　—— 刊臺灣《人間福報》2014.12.2 圖文

彩圖見 93 頁

Oh----how lofty and wonderful
Puyuma----My love forever
Can you hear? At every station
The song I hummed----songs like magpies

96. 重生的喜悦

這清晨
這周遭和光的力
這窗外的寧靜這初綻的花兒
我歡喜，我欲將重生。

啊，生命！啊，淚水！
彷若露珠泛著微光
心中洋溢希望
奔流著我斑斕詩想
我展翼，我想吟唱。

拿起筆 ——
只能寫出
感謝這場相會 ——
是你賜給我最慷慨的恩惠！
讓一切變得恬逸歡愉！

後記：2013 年 6 月 17 日至 22 日住院，開刀大手術於四季台安
　　　醫院，特別向方俊能醫師及全體醫護人員致謝。

—— 寫於 2013/6/22 出院日
—— 刊臺灣《人間福報》副刊，2013.7.9.

96. The Joyance of Rebirth

This cool morning
The surrounding and the power from the light
This serenity out of the window
The newly openrd flowers
I am happy, I shall be reborn

Oh,my life! Ah, my tears!
As if the dews glimmering
With hope wavingin my heart
Flowing of my gorgeous poems
I unfold my wings, and I want to sing

Holding my pen---
I can only write
Thanks for this encounter---
You gave me the most generous favor
Let all of mine become joyance

97. 我原鄉的欖仁樹

喔，我原鄉的欖仁樹，
樹中之樹！
你的清碧枝葉，
為何眷顧著我？
在微雨的四月，
你的生命之歌，
使我深深感動。

每日晨昏，
都看你獨步街頭，
在滿月的夜裡，
在禪那的護念中移足。

喔，我的欖仁樹啊，
每當與你同在
就忘卻外界的煩囂，
祢是台東站前最美麗的一景，
那兒有百鳥的啼囀，
清風、群山和雲彩
我無比的豐足與幸福。

—— 2013.7.1
—— 刊臺灣《乾坤》詩刊第 67 期，2013.07 秋季號
—— 臺灣《笠》詩刊第 296 期，2013.8.15

97. *Tropical Almond Tree in My Hometown*

Oh, tropical almond of my hometown
The King of the trees!
Your green branches and leaves
Always protect me
In drizzling April
Your song of life
Makes me deeply moved

Every morning and dusk
I see you standing alone in the street
Under the full moon at night
You move in the protection of the Dhyana.

O, my tropical almond tree
Whenever I stay with you
I forget all my troubles outside
You are the most beautiful view
In front of the TaiDong station
There are twitterings of the birds
Cool breeze, mountains and clouds
I feel extremely rich and happy

98. 致雙溪

夜霧彌漫小山城，
雙溪河在我眼底喧響。
風依舊蕭索，
送來一地的寒。
那叢綠中的野薑花，
彷彿來自星群，
從平林橋下的親水公園
飛出無數白蝶，
飛向水田
飛向和悅清澈的鏡面。
忽地，一隻孤鷺飛進我的愁緒。
而明天
陽光將仍在花間跳舞，
這鄉景的光華，
寂靜，如秋。

—— 2013.4.25
—— 刊臺灣《乾坤》詩刊第 67 期，
　　2013.07 秋季號

98. To the Double Brook

Night fog pervading the small mountain town
The Double Brook is noicy in front of me
The wind is still bleaking
Bringing the cold to the ground around
The wild ginger flower among the green
As if coming from the stars in the sky
From Qinshui Park under the Pinglin Bridge
Countless white butterflies flying
Flying to the paddy fields
Flying to the harmonious, clean mirror
Suddenly, a lonely heron flies into my melancholy
But tomorrow
Sunshine would still dance among the flowers
The brilliance of the town
Silent, like autumn

99. 坐在秋陽下

坐在秋陽下
就這樣不慌不忙地
聽著木琴聲
我忽然明白了一些事

原來生命像只風箏
雖然微不足道
仍想放飛到高空
看看自己想要什麼
然而，金光依然柔媚
剛灑在油桐樹上
這部落的心跳還在這裡
就像以前那樣，是我溫暖的歸屬

—— 2013.8.30
—— 刊臺灣《人間福報》副刊，
2013.9.23

99. *Sitting Under the Autumn Sun*

Sitting Under the Autumn Sun
Uunhurriedly
Listen to the sound of xylophone
I suddenly understand something

Life is like a kite
Although tiny and small
Still want to fly high to the sky
Have a look at what you want
However, gold light is still soft
Just splashing over the tung trees
The tribe's heart is still throbing
Just like before, is my warm home

100. 海 影

第一次被你感動
我很難説清
在你燦爛的光痕
我以為世上並無如此美好的真情
是風的呼喚
讓我們因緣際會
想讓你認出了我
就忘了國與國的距離
有什麼差別

當我喜愛這一切 ——
棕櫚樹和沙灘、詩集
音樂
啊，島嶼一望無際
如何能留住你的身影
月亮啊，請不要再多説
我只信眼前所聞
一次相遇肯定不夠
在灰藍、灰藍的星群上
明天，請為我們打開希望之門

註：作者於 2013 年十月下旬參訪馬來西亞第 33 屆世詩會，看到
　　各國國旗並列於海面上，蘇丹王子及州長、市長、諾貝爾獎
　　得主 Dr.kahan 等名人前來祝詞，有感而文。
　　　—— 2013.11.6
　　　—— 刊臺灣《人間福報》副刊，2013.11.18

100. Shadow of the Sea

The first time I was moved by you
It's hardly to say
In your brilliant light
I didn't believe
There is such a nice feeling in the world
It 's the calling of the wind
Let us meet by destiny
I hope you could recognize me
I wish we could forget the distance between nations
What is the difference
When I love all of these
Palm trees, sea beach, and poetry
Music
Ah, the island stretches to the horizon
How to keep your silhouette long
Oh, the moon, please don't say any more
I only believe what I have seen now
One meeting is certainly not enough
In the blue -gray constellation
Tomorrow, please open the door of hope for us

101. 東隆宮街景

在這兒，我感到
寒氣不再滯留
瞥見的景物為數眾多
陽光如是輕盈
旁人之目不曾冷漠

在喧鬧時刻的伴唱前
我感謝
過去的幸福與自由
我獨自傾聽到
街人滿是歡悅的幽默

註：東隆宮主祀溫府千歲，是多數東港人的信仰中心。溫王爺姓
溫，名鴻，字德修，東港人慣稱為「王爺公」，信徒多
相信王爺是為地方造福，祈望「東」港興「隆」，
遂命名為「東隆宮」。東港迎王，俗稱東港燒王船，每
三年一科的燒王船，也是屏東縣極富盛名的宗教盛事與文化
祭典。

—— 2013.12.3
—— 刊臺灣《笠》詩刊，第 299 期，2014.02

101. Street View of Donglong Palace

Here, I feel
The chilliness is no longer there
Countless views in front of me
The sunshine is so light
The eyesights of people also warm

Before the bustling of singing
I show my thanks
To the happiness and freedom in the past
I alone hear
Pedestrians are delighted and humourous

102. 北風散步的小徑上

瑩白的夜，溜過原野
顫顫地在風裡翩動
遠處是九梅樹橋
繡著一條碧澄的河階

在部落；一片青樹黃花
倒影於香馥的回頭灣
但等著吧
等吧，這可是藍色的黎明

在回唱？在久久站立的
曙光中北風散步的小徑上
四面裡的
微茫，如海波
流轉著曠野盡頭的彷徨

當半邊隱滅的星劃過長空
垂落的雲氣，水波不興
我的愛在熙攘之外
遺落的足印，清冷不滅

—— 2009.10.29
—— 刊香港《橄欖葉》詩報，第 7 期，2014.06

102. The Lane on Which North Wind Walks

Sparklining and crystal-clear white night
Gliding through the wild
Quivering and tripping moves in the wind
Beyond the bridge of Nine Plums Tree
Embroidered a green jade river rank

Inside the tribe,
A Piece of green trees and yellow flowers
Inverted images in fragrant Bay of Huitouwan Please wait
Wait, for the blue dawn

Answering the singing,
Long standing on the narrow lane
Here the northwind iswalking in dawn

All around
Delicate light, like waves of the sea
Circling the unrest of the end of the moor

When the half hidden star gliding away
The falling clouds, the gentle waves
My love is outside the bustling
The lost footsteps , cold and immortal

103. 葛根塔拉草原之戀

雖然不是我的故土，
卻讓我遐思萬千，
草原未曾衰老，
胡楊憂傷如前。

每當盛夏之季，
野馬賓士勝似行雲，
營盤歌舞宛如嘉年華會，
駝鈴響過逐香之路，
神州飛船鑲入眼簾。

馬頭琴在帳外的蒼茫中浮動，
傳說中的傳說使我迷戀，
這是天堂的邊界，還是繆斯的樂園？
還是我無言的讚歎枯守著期盼的誓約。

103. Song of Gegen Tara Prairie

Though it's not my homeland
I'm fascinated and dream for
The prairie will never wither
The dolorous poplars always there

Whenever the summer comes
Broncos run like swifting clouds
Party dances like carnival gathering
Bell of camels jingling all the way
Airships rising from here up to the sky

Music of Horse Head Fiddle drifting afar
outside the tents
The old tales of the legends intoxicated me
Is this the edge of the paradice,
or the garden of the Muse
Or my silent admiration by the expecting vow

註：集寧師院田智院長 2014.5.20mail 邀請至「烏蘭察布市」一
　　遊，因好奇於地名之奇特，於蒙古語意為「紅色的山崖」，
　　遂有感而文。該市是中國通往蒙古國、俄羅斯和東歐的重要
　　國際通道，全年平均氣溫 4.3 度，人口約 272 萬人。著名的
　　景點「葛根塔拉草原」的蒙古語意為「避暑盛地」，每年農
　　曆五月十三，當地的草原人民都會舉行蒙古族傳統的「祭敖
　　包」活動。據悉，北宋詩人歐陽修曾在一首詩中這樣寫道：
　　「奚琴本出奚人樂，奚人彈之雙淚落」。這奚琴就是現在的
　　馬頭琴。

　　　　　　　── 2014.5.21 作
　　　　　　　── 刊內蒙古《集寧師範學院》2014.03 期，
　　　　　　　　　總第 126 期封底。
　　　　　　　── 刊《人間福報》副刊圖文，2015.3.17

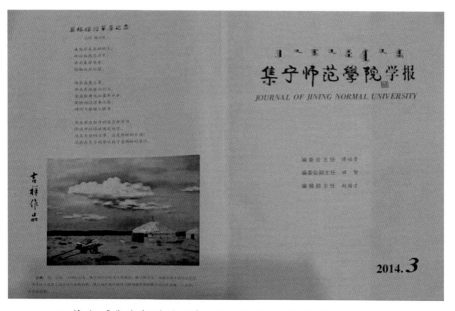

內蒙古《集寧師範學院》2014.03 期，總第 126 期封底。

104. 無論是過去或現在

無論是過去或現在：湛藍和青草、
巨石與白浪、燈塔與鷗鳥，
當我喜愛這一切，
喜愛玻璃船和俏皮的梅花鹿，
而自以為是在天涯海角；

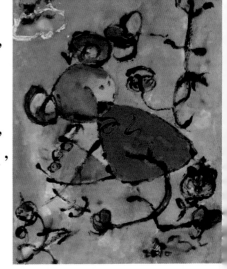

當我移動腳步，直想靠近
這綠島與沙灘，岩洞與山丘，
人權紀念碑前的往事和滄桑歷史，
已然隨著時間慢慢蒸散了；

當我仰天獨自遐想，
就像永久地等待一
允諾我的時間老人，
我們才剛剛相遇，甚至不願離開。

> 註：綠島原名火燒島，是一座位於台東縣外海、太平洋中的海島，
> 行政上屬台東縣綠島鄉；島內山丘縱橫，東南臨海處多為斷
> 崖，西南角是長達十多公里的平原沙灘。島內有溫泉、觀音
> 洞、鹿場、巨岩奇石、林投樹林、燈塔、白沙灘等景點。原
> 是關政治犯的監獄，如今已改為「綠島人權文化園區」的「綠
> 洲山莊」。

　　—— 2014.6.5
　　—— 刊臺灣《人間福報》副刊圖文，2014.11.14

104. No Matter in the Past or at the Present

No matter in the past or at the present
The sky blue and grass green
Huge stones and white waves
Lighthouses and hagdons
when l love it all
I lve the glass boats and nifty sika deer
l imagine l'm in the ultima Thule

When I moved my steps, approaching
The green island and beaches, caves and hills
The past events of memorial of human rights
and the changes of history
All disappeared with the passing time

When l look up at the sky alone thinking
As if I have been waiting a long time----
For the promise from the old man Time
We just meet, and reluctant to part

105. 憶友 ── Ernesto Kahan

你可曾諦聽故鄉花海的歌聲，那
榮美而威嚴的花兒
還有撒瑪利亞城，憂傷而平靜的眼眸
忽若愛神的懶散，
又似夜的寂寥。

你含笑在我面前，
滿懷安寧和自由。
那血脈相連的地土，回鄉的渴望
已深入你靈魂之中。
啊，七弦琴的律動 ──

註：1985 年諾貝爾和平獎得主 prof.Ernesto Kahan 在其故鄉以色
　　列拍攝一張照片並傳來電。

── 2014.4.2
── 刊臺灣《笠詩刊》，第 301 期，2013.06，頁 65。
── 臺灣《秋水詩刊》，第 161 期，2014.10
── 英譯刊-美國《poem of the world》， 2014 春季號

105. Recall My friend
── Ernesto Kahan

Did you listen to the singing of the sea
of beautiful and imperial flowers of hometown
And the Samaria with dolorous and quiet eyes
Like the Angus' idlesse
Like the silence of the night

Your smiling in front of me
Full of peace and freedom
The land unites us by the blood
With our yearning for the hometown
Have deeply embedded in your soul
Oh, the rhythm of the heptachord

106. 四草湖中

我聽過天空
嘎嘎這嘎嘎那的雷響，還有
消失卅餘年的烏蚶重回四草湖懷抱
我歡喜，因為我知道寧靜
如這群白鷺
正緊跟著夕陽而且習以為常了
那紅樹林就在前方
映照出深淺不一的藍

不過，我喜愛的
不只是招潮蟹招展在泥灘
或是氣定神凝的彈塗魚
我關注的
其實只有復育的榮耀
我尋覓，再尋覓
嘎嘎這嘎嘎那的雷響，我用心觀察 ——
並沉湎於最遠那閃光的河道

註：四草位於台南市安南區，以擁有豐富的紅樹林、濕地景觀、
　　水鳥及觀光竹筏、吊罾等著名。2009 年成立的「台江國家
　　公園」內的四草湖，據自由時報 2014.6.5 報導，因水質變好，
　　俗稱「烏蚶」的歪簾蛤在消失卅餘年後，又重新回到四草湖，
　　遂有感而作。

　　　　　　　　　　—— 2014.6.10
　　　　　　　　　　—— 刊《臺灣時報》，2015.3.1
　　　　　　　　　　——《秋水》詩刊，163 期，2015.4

106. In the Sicao Lake

I've heard from the sky
The rumbling thunder, and
Seeing 30 years-disappeared birds and cockles
Back to the embrace of the lake
I'm delighted, because I enjoy the calmness
Like the flock of egrets
Following the setting sun as usual
The mangrove right ahead
Reflecting the different shades of blue colour

Yet, what I love
Is not only the fiddler crabs flaunting in the mudflat
Or the mudskippers lying calm and still
What I care for is only
The glory of restoration
I search, keep on searching
The rumbling thunder, I observe with care —
And indulging in the farthest glittering river

107. 那年冬夜

你的憂懼巨大
而蜷伏
我的恰似
月下草上失足的孤星

生命
正從身邊溜過
什麼時候我重生
哪裡是我夢中的雲影

我們的記憶
是淺鑄的
一面
淚鏡

—— 2014.8.30
—— 刊臺灣《海星詩刊》2014.12 冬季號，
　　第 14 期，頁 94

107. The Winter Night that Year

Your apprehension great
Curling up
Mine is just like
A lonely star dropped on the grassland at night

Life
Is just sliping away by my side
When shall I be reborn
Where will be the shadow of clouds in my dream

Our memory
Is shallowly casted
One
Mirror of tears

108. 知本之夜

沿著坡道而上
盡是流水聲
藍紫交疊的
天空 —— 你提醒著
那向我走來的世界

小鎮空氣中
硫磺
是
揮之不去的記憶
而那星子間訴說的
卑南傳奇
也一路嚼著苦澀氣息

只有我
把伏在山丘上的月
顫顫地
捧起
在隔窗貧困的夜下

註：知本位於台東市西南郊 17 公里處，因溫泉及森林遊樂區等
　　自然景觀而盛名。區內原住民計有卑南族、魯凱族、排灣族
　　等族群。　　　　　　　　　　　　　 —— 2012.2.1 作

　　 —— 刊臺灣《笠》詩刊，第 295 期，2013 年 6 月。

108. *Night of Zhiben*

Along the slope climbing up
All ears the sound of flowing water
The blue and the purple mixed
Sky---you remind me
The world coming to me

In the air of the small town
Sulfur
Is
The unforgettable memory
And the explanation in between the stars
The lacal Legents of the tribes
Is chawing with bitter smell

Only me
Quiveringly
Holding
The moon
Subsiding on the hill
Under the pale night by the window

109. 月桃記憶

每年秋末
月桃花綴滿山野
當果實迸裂
種子又散落山谷時
我總會想起
那一天
在東部濱海的
都蘭部落
我看到
一個個專注編織的老人
在這靜寂的園子
歡迎我

她們高興就唱得甜蜜
偶爾也會皺著眉頭
檳榔和酒香
就成共同的慰藉

她們將曬乾的月桃葉
一片片剝開

109. Memory of Moon Peach Blossoms

Every late autumn
Moon peach blossoms full of mountains
When fructifications split
Seeds scattering in the valley
I always remember
That day
By eastern coast
The Du Lan tribe
I see
Old ladies concentrating on knitting
In the quiet garden
Welcoming me

They sing songs sweetly when they are happy
Occasionally they frown
Betel nuts and fragrant wine
Become their common comfort

They peel the sun-baked leaves of peach blossoms
One piece after another

捲成圓圈圈
再曬一次
開始編織成籃子或手提包

這是後山的傳奇嗎
我好奇又興奮地問
美麗的鳥兒啊，告訴我
這周圍的一切
不是夢
那月桃記憶
恰如夜半更深的輕喚親吻
沒有歌詞，卻永不消逝

註：自古以來月桃就深具有民俗味，可用月桃葉包粽子；加以魯
　　凱族、卑南族和阿美族人多會用月桃葉為編織材料。葉鞘可
　　當繩索，莖梗一片片剝開曬乾後，就是「月桃編」的材料。
　　她們將之卷成圓圈圈，再曬一次，其堅韌程度並不遜於竹
　　藤，且葉子更易於彎曲。接著，再以錯綜交織的手法編成背
　　籃、草席、坐墊、手提袋、搖籃等日常用具。尤以月桃葉織
　　成的草席，有冬暖夏涼的作用。

—— 2013.1.10
—— 刊中國澳門《華文百花》2013.01，
　　期總第 18 期，2013.08
—— 刊臺灣《人間福報》副刊，2013.7.2
　　刊登圖文

Rolled them into circles
Dried in the sun once again
Then to weave them into baskets or handbags

Is this the legend from the back mountain
I ask them curiously and excitedly
Beautiful bird, please tell me
Everything here around
It is not a dream
The memory of moon peach blossoms
Just like the gentle calling and kisses at night
No lyrics, but never disappear

110. 想妳，在墾丁

每年落山風吹起
是墾丁旅遊的淡季
但我總會想起妳
如同孤鳥
整夜不眠地徘徊在
月光覆蓋的礁岩上

當我拾起貝殼，貼進耳裡
我就感到驚奇，彷彿
那座軍艦石潛過大海
瞧，妳長髮如樹冠的葉片般
柔美而飄逸
瞬間，如夏雨

蘇鐵睡眠著、白野花兒睡眠著
甚至連星兒也那樣熟睡了
只有沉默的島嶼對我們說話 ——
就讓時間蒼老吧
這世界已有太多東西逝去
我只想擁有自然、夜，和珍貴的友誼

註：屏東墾丁除有沙灘美景外，更被列為世界十大熱帶植物園，
有著自然保留區保護的高位珊瑚礁植群。　　　—— 2013.12.24
　　—— 刊臺灣《秋水》詩刊，第 162 期，2015.01，頁 26。

110. I Miss You, at Kending

Every year when the northern-east wind blowing
It is the slack for traveling in Kending
But I shall alsway remember you
Like a lonely bird
The whole sleepless night lingering
On the moonlight covered reefs

When I pick up one shell, put it to my ears
I would always feel the wonder, as if
That rock of warship shaped moving in the sea
See, your long hair like leaves of crown of a tree
Gentle, beautiful and elegant
In a blink, like raining in summer
Cycad trees are asleep, white wild flowers are asleep
Even the stars are also sound asleep
Only the silent island talks to us----
Let the time getting old
Too many things in the world disappear
I only want to hold the nature, the night, and
The valuable friendship

111. 冬日神山部落

冬日大武山的寧靜裡
有神秘清昂的魔力：
柔和的光澤與雀榕樹的斑斕，
院牆小貓慵懶的哈欠聲；
霧嬝嬝的岩板巷，
環繞部落孤遺的地……
有時一隻五色鳥飛起，
宛若預告幸福的閃現，
又像是萬物靜止的終點。
我在魯凱族孩童身上
找回生命中不悔的歡愉。

— 2014.12.17
— 刊臺灣《秋水》詩刊，第 162 期，
　　2015.01，頁 26。

111. Winter Days in Koyama Tribe

Peaceful winter days in Dawu mountain
There is a mysterious magic power :
Gentle light, gorgeous leaves of Sparrow Banyan
Little cat yawning by the wall of the courtyard
The fogging lane of rocky planks

The isolated field circling the tribe-----

Sometimes one colourful bird flying
As if to foretell the flashing happiness
Also like the end of the stillness of the world
From the children of Rukai tribe
I find out the regretless merriness and joy

112. 恬　靜

濱海公園旁海灣澹澹，
漁舟猶有奮力駛去的波紋，
我迷惑地望著遠方，
竟如此幸福，恬靜而溫暖！
瞧那橄欖青的、迷濛的
藍，還有浪花乍現 —— 隨之喝采
特別是泊在岸沿的
雀鳥像神仙般
—— 接力地喧響，用喜悅替後山上彩。

—— 2015.1.24
—— 《臺灣時報》，2015.3.1，圖文

112. Serenity

Drifting water of the bay by the Binhai park
Repples of fishing boats shooting out
With puzzles I look afar
Unexpectedly feel so happy, quiet and warm
See that olive- coloured , misty
Blue, the flowers of waves present, ——
Following the cheers
Especially what berthed by the shore
The birds like angels
—— relaying for the echoing
Adding colour of joy to the back mountain

附錄一

1985 年諾貝爾和平獎得主 prof. Ernesto Kahan 翻譯 Dr.Lin Ming-Li 的一首詩及 mail 留念

Iniciemos nuestra comunicación
Apoya tu mano sobre la mía!

http://www.youtube.com/watch?v=sc8LPtZ5Q98

prof. Ernesto Kahan　--1985 諾貝爾和平獎得主

左起：林明理、prof. Ernesto Kahan、印度詩人

1985 年諾貝爾和平獎得主 Prof. Ernesto Kahan 於
故鄉以色列拍攝，贈與作者。

如果你立在冬雪裡

如果你立在冬雪裡
用沾濕的眼眸
向我端視
猶如抖落羽葉的風
等待
春日的小小呵欠

啊史迪威，我的永念
為什麼歸程屢屢橫阻
為什麼冷雨頻頻滴淚
難道你聽不見
我的默喚似小舟
緩緩地盪著　　漾著

如果我立在交錯晃影的地鐵裡
　或癡望原野上
只要有你，只要有你的展顏
　哪怕星光不語
哪怕月兒隱遁
你就是篇溫和的詩章，如菖蒲般綠

　　　　—— 2011.12.24 作
　　　　—— 刊《笠詩刊》，288 期，2012.04

De pie en la nieve del invierno

Si de pie estás en la nieve del invierno
mírame
con los ojos húmedos
como si el viento sacudiendo una pluma
esperando
el bostezo ligero de la primavera

Oh, Stilwel, mi eterno recuerdo
Por qué el viaje a casa siempre se acorralada?
Por qué las lluvias frías persisten con lágrimas
No puedo escuchar
Mi silencio es como un pequeño bote
quieto, remando y remando

Si estoy en el entrelazado y danzante metro
o busco obsesionada en el campo silvestre
y sólo tú estuvieras aquí, mostrando tu cara
incluso si las estrellas no hablaran
incluso si la luna se ocultara
tu serías el cálido poema, tan verde como el cálamo

If You Stand in the Winter Snow

If you stand in the winter snow
Look at me
With your wet eyes
As if the wind shaking off the feather
Waiting
The slight yawning of the spring time

Oh, Stilwel, my everlasting memory
Why the journey to home always blocked
Why the cold rains keep on with tears
Can t you hear
My silent calling like a small boat
Quietly rowing, and rowing

If I stand in the interleaving and dazzing subway
Or look into the wild field obsessed
If only you are here,
If only you show your face here
Even if the stars not speaking
Even if the moon is hidden
You will be the warm poem,as green as the calamus

2013 年 11 月 19 日於 10:27 PM

Dear friend Lin Ming-Li

Thanks for your superb poems. I love them!!!

Here is the translation of one into Spanish （ What Stilwel is?）

Love and friendship

Ernesto Kahan

Dearest Lin Ming li

Thanks a lot for the photos of you and I in the newspaper .

Have you happy holidays and a very successful and alive year 2014 full of happiness, love and poetry and that the friendship that unites us will continue.

Ernesto

Sent: Tuesday, December 03, 2013 2:32 AM

To: Prof. Ernesto Kahan

附錄二

富岡海堤小吟

我在海上擁抱渴望
世界已無關緊要
且讓我拾一枚思索之果
望一舟從遠古攜浪而來

啊，加路蘭港 ──
多少星轉斗移
全在夢幻裡
留下一聲浩嘆

啊，逝者如斯
多少生生靈靈
全在歲月裡
隨風飄向你的襟懷

是誰穿透一部詩史
讓我悠悠思念

這藍碧的水，稀微的風與
白色的光

註：富岡漁港位於臺東市與卑南鄉交界的附近，是臺東縣內第二
　　大之漁港，僅次於成功漁港。漁港興建於 1954 年，原名「加
　　路蘭港」，因鄰近阿美族部落「加路藍社」而得名。

　　　　　　　── 2014.4.8 作
　　　　　　　── 刊臺灣《笠詩刊》，第 301 期，
　　　　　　　　　2013.06，頁 65-66。

附錄三
傷悼 ── 前鎮氣爆受難者

有某種寒意
在港都黃昏
穿透，如厝鳥仔哀嚎
鼓盪 ──
卻又凝定靜止。

慢慢地，大地開始振作，
慢慢地，風撫平了傷痕；
除了踟躕的太陽
僵持驚視的姿勢。

啊，落潮如此
為何默不作聲？
那層怪異的氣體，修復得了嗎？
為何雨微微地哭 ──
你已在夢中逝水般流逝

── 2014.8.2 作
── 刊臺灣《人間福報》副刊圖文，2014.8.18

附錄四

勇者的畫像 ── 致綠蒂

天上的雲啊，和我一樣
秋光的飄泊者
我們源自同一故鄉
那兒有閃耀的蔗田，懷舊的小巷
那兒有蟬嘶的童年，華燈的廟堂
從銀河的北面奔向南方

是誰驅趕著你？
遊牧的行吟？命運的神話？
鄉愁的悸動？曠原的呼喊？
或是駐留使你倦怠？
是不息的血脈相連的山？
還是一生深長的眷想？

噢，不，你已棲息靈魂中……
歌聲在星夜中倍感清妙
那曾經的華麗與愁悵
已幻成合掌的真誠
隨著鐘鼓、海風，喜悅飛翔
你沒有行腳，無所謂陽光

── 2013.10.29
── 刊臺灣《秋水詩刊》，161 期，
　　2014.10.

附錄五

蘿蔔糕

在鯉魚山市集
我瞥見了 ——
　　腦海中的畫面
那是蘿蔔糕
在爐灶上
四溢。

每逢佳節
我常吮吸著
那怦然的氣味
貼進大地風是甜的
勤奮的母親輕煽著
　　　柴火⋯⋯

而月彎垂，透過
半開的　木門
還有夢中雞啼 ——

啊，童年
記憶已成斑駁
我不得不重新刷新

註：蘿蔔糕的台灣話稱為「菜頭粿」，客家語則稱之為蘿蔔粄或
　　菜頭粄；在華人或新加坡、甚至東亞地區為普遍的美食。文
　　中的鯉魚山位於台東舊火車站旁，在早市攤位中，驚見有位
　　婦人素來以賣蘿蔔糕為生，遂而喚起了記憶。印象中，母親
　　將在來米洗淨泡水，隔夜再用石磨製成米漿，又把白蘿蔔去
　　皮刨絲，加水再入鍋悶煮至蘿蔔軟爛。再將原米漿倒入炒菜
　　鍋中，加入蘿蔔絲及蘿蔔湯汁，並以鹽巴和胡椒調味。開小
　　火後，須不停翻拌，直到變成米糊，再攪拌成炒不動的米糰。
　　最後填入圓型蒸籠中。待涼脫模，可感覺到，一種原樸的味
　　道。母親會切塊煎香，食用時，沾些西螺丸莊醬油膏或甜辣
　　醬。天冷時，還可將之切成條狀，用高湯煮，加些香菇、芹
　　菜及茼蒿，十分可口。可惜這傳統的作法已漸消失，只能到
　　記憶中去尋覓了。

—— 2014.9.4 作
—— 刊臺灣《臺灣時報》台灣文學版，
　　2014.9.18.圖文

附錄六

流　浪　漢

他，來自花蓮⋯⋯一個流浪漢 ── 孤單的晃影擋住了我。

疲憊的、無助的步伐，一把雨傘、簡易的背包。哎 ── 怎麼說呢？──

掩翳的傷口，自慚形穢的腳丫，透出情怯的神色⋯⋯

呵，不必多說，這個不幸的人，還有那跋涉的荊棘路，讓我費神許久。

我摸索自己的口袋⋯⋯只掏出錢包裡的一張大鈔、一罐飲料，

加上一包糧食，甚至不好意思握住那只厚實的手。

「哦，兄弟，我這點心意。別客氣 ── 神會眷顧你的！」

那就是我最後看到他轉身離去、月光照亮在柏油路上的時候。

不過 ── 可能嗎？這天氣是越加寒涼了。遠處，還有狗吠的聲音。

他該回到家中的小屋了吧。今天去應徵的那家果園面試得如何？

「大姐，謝謝妳。但，我想，還是留在這附近再找找工

作啦……。」

　　他靦腆地說道，聲音來自遙遠的一方、有雜訊干擾著。

　　「喂喂……喂哪兒的話呀。」我急急地回覆。哎他手機沒電了吧。

　　而我終於了悟，失去一切，對他而言，還不算災難。

　　因為，他天天思念，那熟悉的牧場，牛羊成群，還有一整片綠原。

　　　　註：今年九月，巧遇了一位因工作九年的牧場突然關閉而失業的
　　　　　　原住民流浪到台東求職未成，遂而折回花蓮繼續謀職的坎坷
　　　　　　故事，有感而作。

　　　　　── 21014.10.6
　　　　　── 圖文刊臺灣《臺灣時報》，臺灣文學版，2014.10.12

附錄七
竹子湖之戀

　　霧裊裊在斜坡上，在竹子湖附近嬉戲不歇……當我把耳朵貼進七星山，我就聽見那百鳥在夢中振翼飛舞的旋律，那些老農在訴說著半生的酸甜，那蓬萊米原鄉的故事和不斷起伏稻浪的和絃。

　　台北樹蛙鳴叫，珍貴而奇美，在水池邊跳躍。樹蟬用盡力氣嘶鳴了整個夏天。當月光灑落小油坑前，一種富於音樂性的思想忽地而起，在天籟中交織 —— 啊，飛去吧，—— 那兒有沉睡中的夢土，風、海芋和清泉。

　　在這樣的夜，一樣的露水，啊，我甦醒，而空茫之景如水。也許那兒的光和可遇不可求的秀麗又鐫刻心動，—— 只為人間，而我徜徉在這島嶼東緣，在眼睛明暗交接處迎出了樹影靜怡後的思念。　　　　　　—— 2014.6.17 於台東

　　　　　　—— 刊臺灣《人間福報》副刊圖文，2014.10.24

附錄八

北國的白樺

── 致北京大學謝冕教授

北國的白樺
矗立崖上，
群雁親近
向它丈量。

如星光照影
在疾風中，──
昂首而歌
讓夜驚嘆。

人們鍾愛它
面容安詳，
我卻欣賞它
誦讀的音響。

── 2013.4.14 作
── 收編古遠清教授編著，《謝
冕評說三十年》，2013 年，
中國，海天出版社。
── 收編譚五昌教授編著，《國
際漢語詩歌》，2013.11，北
京，線裝書局。

附錄九
寫給相湖的歌

　　多美的雲天！在七月的暮影下，月亮灣沙灘竟羞紅了臉，如同繆斯久久凝視的輕俏戀人。

　　鄰鄰湖波，一眼看去，總是歡欣雀躍。漁歌唱晚好像白鷺飛舞。跟搖櫓的吱吱聲不同，此地河道，每每質樸純真。

　　我向相湖莞爾一笑，是愛，讓我們相親相近，這景象便在我心中永存。這裡花香流轉，涼風習習。這裡水域廣闊，更有稻田縱橫，濕地之眼為鄰。

　　然而，置身這江南水鄉中，我瞥見了日復一日的水漲潮落。

　　在一沉靜無垢的湖畔旁，遙思昔日懷家亭館，我就要扮演揮毫的墨客。看盡七星鎮穿梭著寬寬窄窄的河道，看盡這裡的一鄉一景，這清麗婉約所給我的精神至寶。

　　眼睛好似在說：「這就是我羨慕的天堂，這就是友誼和愛戀的地方。」啊，這是一首甜蜜的戀歌。是誰？在黑夜睡夢時將它哼起？是誰？在晨靄漫漫時將它隱沒？是誰歌著「花氣熏人似酒醇，東風隨處掃香塵」的曲調？

　　啊，這支歌曲，帶我飄洋過海，來到湘家蕩，感受她不朽的面貌！相湖──我願隨風與妳嬉舞！與妳共呼吸。哎，

要是有一只翅羽。

　　這樣的夜，一樣的露水，啊，我甦醒，而妳像一隻佛眼，早已閱盡宇宙的奧秘。也許那兒的光和可遇不可求的狂喜又怦然心動，—— 而一種富於音樂性的思想忽地而起，在天籟中交織 —— 啊，飛去吧，—— 那兒有沉睡中的濕地島嶼，古寺和綠地。

　　每當妙曼的月亮在樹梢，在這塊上蒼遺落在長三角腹地的液體翡翠上……當我把耳朵貼進一灣碧水，我就聽到那百鳥在夢中振羽的旋律，那些旅人在盡享水上遊樂，那魚米之鄉的故事和遠方 —— 不斷眨眼的星子如露水一滴。

　　　　　　　　　—— 2014.7.10
　　　　　　　　　—— 獲中外散文詩學會主辦散文詩比賽
　　　　　　　　　　　「榮譽獎」，收入四川省《散文詩
　　　　　　　　　　　世界》，總第 113 期，2014 年.09 期，
　　　　　　　　　　　頁 10。

附錄十
致出版家彭正雄先生

我認得出，你是一介勇士
是風，讓我們聚會
寫作的喜悅
出書的推手
那裡曾是你寄予的希望
書是香的，你也是。

你埋首在鍵盤前，專注無旁的
背影，神情莊重
彷若巨龍親吻著天空。

呵，我期待
你將看到我如何在
永不靜止的起跑
繼續裝飾著我的夢
我還希求什麼，你的書城
就是我最好的寄託。

P.S 感謝文史哲出版社協助出書數冊。
2015.3.26 明理合十於台東

── 刊《臺灣時報》臺灣文學版 2015.4.2

Professor WU Jun

吳鈞教授主要作品：
Professor Wu Jun's Main Publications

學術專著 monograph：

專著：《魯迅詩歌翻譯傳播研究》，臺灣文史哲出版社，2012
年 8 月出版

monograph：《A Study Of Translation And Communication Of
Lu Xun's Poems》, Literature, History And Philosophy
Press,Taiwan, 2012.8.

專著：《魯迅翻譯文學研究》，齊魯書社，2009

monograph: WU Jun, *Study of Lu Xun's Translated Literature*,
Qilu Press, Jinan, 2009.1.

專著：《學思錄 —— 英語教研文集》，內蒙古人民出版社，
1999

monograph: WU Jun, Learning and Thinking-A Collection of
Wu Jun' Papers on English Teaching and Research, Inner
Mongolia People's Press, Hohhot, 1999

the Dream of Gold, Learning and Thinking, 9, 1995

Journals like *Studies of Zhouyi, Qilu Academic Study, Journal
of Northwest Normal University* （Social Sciences） and

Gansu Social Sciences are indexed in Chinese Social Science Citation Index （CSSCI）.

參編書：co- edited books

參編：《譯學詞典與譯學理論文集》，山東大學出版社，2003

Co-editor：Wu Jun*, Anthology of Translatological Dictionaries and Translation Theories,* Shandong University Press, Jinan, 2003

參編：《大學英語精讀 5 級同步輔導與強化》，大連理工學院出版社，1999

Co-editor：Wu Jun, *Teacher's Book of Intensive Reading of College English ,Book 5,* Publishing House of Dalian Institute of Science and Technology, Dalian, 1999

翻譯　Translation:

譯著：《魯迅詩歌全英譯》，臺灣文史哲出版社，2012 年 11 月出版

Translation Work: Lu Xun Complete Poems Literature, History And Philosophy Press,Taiwan, November, 2012..

譯著：吳開豫著詩集《自珍集》，中國文史出版社，2006

Translation of the peotry anthology: Collection of the Poems which I cherish by Wu Kaiyu, China Literature and History Publishing House, Beijing, 2006,

英譯：《吳開晉詩歌選集》團結出版社，2013 年 10 月出版

Translation of the Poetry Collection:Selected Poems of Wu
    Kaijin, Tuanjie Press, October,2013

英譯：林明理《回憶的沙漏》，臺灣秀威出版社，2012 年 2 月

Translation of the Poetry Collection: Sandglass of Memory,
    Showwe Information Co., Ltd. 2012.2.

譯著：臺灣詩歌集《清雨塘》英譯，臺灣文史哲出版社，
    2012,11.

Clear Rain pond, Translation of Collection of the Poems,
    literature, history and philosophy Press,Taiwan, 11，2012,
    Writer: Lin Mingli, Translator: Wu Jun

編譯《老屋的倒塌 ── 愛德格‧愛倫坡驚險故事》，山東文
    藝出版社，2000

The Fall of the House of Usher-The New Edition of Edgar Allan
    Poe's Adventurous Stories, *Shandong Literature and Arts
    Press, Jinan, 2000, Translator: Wu Jun*

漢譯英：林明理詩歌漢譯英臺灣林明理詩歌《雨夜》、《夏
    荷》，《World Poetry Anthology 2010》（2010 第三十
    屆世界詩人大會世界詩選），臺灣，頁 328-331。

Translation of Chinese poem to English: *Rainy Night, Summer
    Lotus* by Lin Mingli, World Poetry Anthology 2010, Page
    328-331.

翻譯吳開晉詩歌"寫在海瑞墓前"、"致瀑布"和"灘
    江"，《老年作家》，第 4 期，2009

In Front of the Tumulus Of Hairui, To Waterfall and *Li River*,

Elderly Writers, 4, 2009, Poet: Wu Kaijin, Translator: Wu Jun

翻譯吳開晉詩歌"椰林歌聲"，香港大型漢英雙語詩學季刊《當代詩壇》2009 年第 51-52 期

Songs in the Coconut Wood, *Contemporary Poetry, 51-52, 2009, Poet: Wu Kaijin,*

Translator: WU Jun

翻譯吳開晉詩歌"久違的雷電"，《當代詩壇》，第 51-52 期，2009

The Long Absent Thunder and Lighting, Contemporary Poetry, 51-52, 2009, Poet: Wu Kaijin, Translator: Wu Jun

翻譯《中國沾化吳氏族譜》序言，中國檔案出版社，2008

Preface of Pedigree of Wu Family Zhuanhua, China Archives Press, Beijing, 2008,

Translator: Wu Jun

翻譯"易理詮釋與哲學創造"，《周易研究》（增刊），2003

Philosophical Creation and Interpretation by Yi Principles, Study of Zhouyi, supplement, 2003, Writer: Gao Ruiquan, Translator: Zhang Wenzhi, Wu Jun

翻譯吳開晉教授詩歌《土地的記憶》，1996，榮獲東京世界詩人大會以色列米瑞姆·林勃哥德詩歌和平獎，後被收入了該國反法西斯戰爭紀念文集中。

The Memory of the Land, 1996, Poet: WU Kaijin, Translator: Wu Jun

This translated poem won Miriam Lindbergin Israel Poetry For

Peace Prize in World Congresses of Poets for the celebration of the 60th Anniversary of the Victories in the Global Anti-fascist War ,1996. Tokyo, Japan. Later it was collected into the festschrift of poems of this country.

美國大型詩歌季刊（世界詩刊）2010 年～2013 年，發表吳鈞英譯臺灣詩人林明理詩約 18 首：

《Poems of the World》of USA, published Wu Jun's translation of Chinese poems from 2010-2013:

Light Dots（光點）、Summer Lotus（夏荷）、Autumn Rain In October（十月秋雨）、Rainy Night（雨夜）、Once（曾經）、The Season OF Yearning（想念的季節）、Fog（霧）、Upon The Stars（在那星星上）、The Night Wind Of April（四月的夜風）、In The White Summer（在白色的夏季裡）、Harbor In autumn days（秋日的港灣）、Midnight（午夜）、Meteor Shower（流星雨）、The Extinction of Grey-faced Buzzards（看灰面鵟鷹消逝）、Morning Fog（早霧）等。

詩人作家林明理博士作品目錄記錄（2007-2015.03）

●中國學術期刊

1. 南京《南京師範大學文學院學報》，2009 年 12 月 30 日出版，總第 56 期，詩評〈簡潔單純的真實抒寫 — 淺釋非馬的詩〉，頁 24-30。

2. 《安徽師範大學學報》人文社會科學版，第 38 卷第 2 期，總第 169 期，2010 年 3 月，詩評〈最輕盈的飛翔 — 淺釋鍾鼎文的詩〉，頁 168-170。

3. 江蘇省《鹽城師範學院學報》人文社會科學版，第 31 卷，總第 127 期，2011.01 期，書評〈簡論吳開晉詩歌的藝術思維〉，頁 65-68。

3-1. 《鹽城師範學院學報》，第 32 卷，總第 138 期，2012 年第 6 期，詩評〈一泓幽隱的飛瀑—淺釋魯迅詩歌的意象藝術〉，頁 44-48。

4. 福建省《莆田學院學報》，第 17 卷，第 6 期，總第 71 期，2010.12，書評〈評黃淑貞《以石傳情 — 談廟宇石雕意象及其美感》〉，頁〈封三〉。

4-1. 《莆田學院學報》，第 19 卷第 1 期，總第 78 期，2012 年 1 月，書評〈禪悅中的慈悲 — 談星雲大師《合掌人

生》，封底頁〈封三〉。

5.湖北省武漢市華中師範大學文學院主辦《世界文學評論》／《外國文學研究》〈AHCI 期刊〉榮譽出品，2011 年 05 月，第一輯〈總第 11 輯〉，頁 76-78。詩評〈真樸的睿智 —— 狄金森詩歌研究述評〉。

5-1 湖北省武漢市《世界文學評論》，第 15 輯，2013 年 05 月第 1 版，，詩評〈論費特詩歌的藝術美〉，頁 42-46。

6.山東省《青島大學學院學報》，第 28 卷，第 2 期，2011 年 6 月，詩評〈一棵冰雪壓不垮的白樺樹 —— 淺釋北島的詩〉，頁 122-124。

7.廣西大學文學院主辦《閱讀與寫作》，總第 322 期，2009.07，書評〈尋找意象與內涵 —— 辛牧在台灣詩壇的意義〉，頁 5-6。

7-1.《閱讀與寫作》，總第 328 期，2010.01，詩評〈讀非馬詩三首〉，頁 8-9。

7-2.《閱讀與寫作》，總第 346 期，2011.07，詩評〈表現生活美學的藝術 —— 台灣「鐵道詩人」錦連的創作〉，頁 31-32。

8.西南大學中國新詩研究所主辦《中外詩歌研究》，2009 年第 2 期，詩評〈「照夜白」的象徵 —— 非馬〉，頁 11-13。

8-1.《中外詩歌研究》，2010 年第 3 期，詩評〈辛牧的詩化人生〉，頁 21-22。

8-2.《中外詩歌研究》，2011 年第 3 期，書評〈書畫中捕捉純真 —— 讀楊濤詩選《心窗》〉，頁 18-19。

8-3.《中外詩歌研究》，2012 年第 01 期，詩評〈一棵挺立的孤松 —— 淺釋艾青的詩〉，頁 17-24。

9.江蘇省社會科學院主辦《世界華文文學論壇》，2009 年第
　4 期，總第 69 期，詩評〈商禽心理意象的詩化 —— 淺釋
　《逃亡的天空》〉，頁 60-61。

9-1.《世界華文文學論壇》，2010 年第 3 期，總第 72 期，
　　書評〈鞏華詩藝美學的沉思〉，頁 45-46。

9-2.《世界華文文學論壇》，2011 年第 2 期，總第 75 期，
　　詩評〈鄭愁予詩中的自然意象與美學思維〉，頁 49-51。

9-3.《世界華文文學論壇》，2012 年第 4 期，總第 81 期，
　　詩評〈夢與真實的雙向開掘 —— 淺釋蘇紹連的詩〉，頁
　　18-20。

9-4.《世界華文文學論壇》，2013 年第 2 期，總第 83 期，
　　詩評〈一泓深碧的湖水 —— 讀彭邦楨的詩〉，頁 18-20。

10. 上海市魯迅紀念館編《上海魯迅研究》，2011 夏，上海
　　社會科學院出版社，書評〈概觀魯迅翻譯文學研究〉有
　　感〉，頁 244-250。

10-1 《上海魯迅研究》，2013 春，上海社會科學院出版社，
　　書評〈評吳鈞的《魯迅詩歌翻譯傳播研究》，頁 199-201。

11.河南省《商丘師範學院學報》，第 28 卷，2012 年第 1 期，
　　總第 205 期，書評〈論丁旭輝的《台灣現代詩中的老莊
　　身影與道家美學實踐》，頁 22-23。

11-1. 河南省《商丘師範學院學報》，2013 年第 1 期，詩評
　　〈論周夢蝶詩中的道家美學 —— 以《逍遙遊》、《六月》
　　為例〉，頁 24-27。

12.寧夏省《寧夏師範學院學報》，2012.第 02 期，第 33 卷，
　　總第 160 期，詩評〈愛倫‧坡的詩化人生〉。

13.全國中文核心期刊山東省優秀期刊《時代文學》，2009

年第 2 期，總第 149 期，書封面刊登「特別推薦林明理」，刊新詩共 19 首〈小鴨〉〈秋收的黃昏〉〈煙雲〉〈獨白〉〈瓶中信〉〈牧羊女的晚禱〉〈山間小路〉〈冬盡之後〉〈我願是一片樹海〉〈夏荷〉〈愛是一種光亮〉〈無言的讚美〉〈笛在深山中〉〈寒風吹起〉〈畫中花〉〈萊斯河向晚〉〈在初冬湖濱〉〈老樹〉〈青煙〉，頁 63-65。

13-1. 《時代文學》，2009 年第 6 期，總第 157 期封面特別推介作者名字，散文 1 篇〈山城之旅〉及作品小輯，詩評非馬、辛牧、商禽、大荒共 4 文〉，頁 23-31。

13-2. 《時代文學》，2009 年第 12 期，總第 169 期，封面特別推介作者名字於「理論、評論版」，詩評〈讀辛鬱〈豹〉〈鷗和日出〉〈風〉〉、〈讀牛漢〈落雪的夜〉〈海上蝴蝶〉〉、〈商禽心理意象與詩化〉共 3 文，頁 33-38。

14. 內蒙古《集寧師範學院學報》，2013 年第 2 期，第 35 卷，總第 121 期，頁 1-5。書評〈讀盧惠餘《聞一多詩歌藝術研究》〉。

14-1. 內蒙古《集寧師範學院學報》，2014 年第 3 期，第 36 卷，總第 126 期，頁 7-10。評論〈陳義海詩歌的思想藝術成就〉。及刊於封二新詩一首〈葛根塔拉草原之戀〉。

●中國詩文刊物暨報紙

1.北京中國人民大學主辦《當代文萃》，2010.04，發表詩 2 首〈雲淡了，風清了〉〈縱然剎那〉。

2.山東省作家協會主辦《新世紀文學選刊》月刊，2009 年 08 期，刊作者封面水彩畫及詩評二章〈張默詩三首的淺釋〉〈周夢蝶的詩《垂釣者》與藝術直覺〉，頁 58-61。

2-1. 山東《新世紀文學選刊》月刊，2009 年 11 期，刊封面畫及新詩 2 首〈崖邊的流雲〉〈從海邊回來〉，頁 24-25。

2-2. 山東《新世紀文學選刊》月刊，2009 增刊，刊封面畫及新詩 1 首〈星河〉，頁 123。

2-3. 山東《新世紀文學選刊》月刊，2010 年 01 期刊封面畫及詩評 2 篇〈讀丁文智的《鎖定》、《芒》、《自主》〉，〈讀管管詩〉，頁 56-59。

2-4. 山東《新世紀文學選刊》月刊，2010 年 03 期刊封面畫及林明理詩選 9 首〈懷舊〉〈凝〉〈穿越〉〈四月的夜風〉〈原鄉-咏六堆〉〈每當黃昏飄進窗口〉〈樹林入口〉〈北埔夜歌〉〈曾經〉，頁 17-18。

2-5. 山東《新世紀文學選刊》月刊，2011 增刊，刊林明理詩作〈黃昏是繆斯沉默的眼神…〉〈回憶〉〈藍色的眼淚〉〈在黑暗的平野上〉〈懷鄉〉〈紗帽山秋林〉〈密林〉〈在我深深的足跡上〉，頁 131-132。

2-6. 山東省《新世紀文學選刊》自 2009.01 至 2010.03 該刊物封面畫刊登林明理水彩畫作彩色版共 15 幅。詳見 http://mall.cnki.net/magazine/magalist/XSHS.htm

3.河北省作家協會主辦《詩選刊》，2008 年 9 月，總第 287 期，刊作者簡介照片及新詩 4 首，〈夜思〉〈草露〉〈秋復〉〈十月秋雨〉，頁 24。

3-1.《詩選刊》，2009 年 7 月，總第 307 期，刊作者簡介照片及書評綠蒂《春天記事》，頁 94-96。

3-2.《詩選刊》，2010 年 04 月，總第 324 期，刊詩 2 首〈夏荷〉〈小雨〉。

4.新疆省石河子文聯主辦、優秀社科期刊《綠風》詩刊，2009

年第 3 期刊作者簡介照片及新詩 7 首〈夜思〉〈江岸暮色〉〈山茶〉〈老紫藤〉〈遲來的春天〉〈春風,流在百草上〉〈想念的季節〉,頁 102-104。

4-1.《綠風》詩刊,2010 年第 3 期,刊新詩〈四月的夜風〉〈二○○九年冬天〉〈光點〉,頁 41-42。

5.遼寧省作協主辦《詩潮》一級期刊,2009 年 12 月,總第 162 期,刊詩 2 首〈星河〉〈四月的夜風〉,頁 76。

5-1.《詩潮》一級期刊,2010 年 2 月,總第 164 期刊詩 2 首〈崖邊的流雲〉〈青藤花〉,頁 64。

5-2.《詩潮》一級期刊,2011 年 05 月,總第 179 期,刊目錄前作家來訪臺文化交流合照〈做者於後排左三〉。

6.香港詩歌協會《圓桌詩刊》,第 26 期,2009 年 9 月,發表詩評 1 篇〈清逸中的靜謐—讀余光中《星之葬》、《風鈴》〉,頁 94-98,新詩 2 首〈春已歸去〉〈流螢〉頁 27。

6-1.《圓桌詩刊》,第 33 期,2011 年 9 月,刊詩評 1 篇「楊澤的詩〈人生不值得活的〉」頁 64-66,作者簡介及新詩 2 首〈早霧〉〈十月煙海〉頁 26-27。

6-2.《圓桌詩刊》,第 38 期, 2012 年 12 月,詩評 1 篇〈詩人秀實肖像〉頁 62-63,及作者簡介。

7.香港《香港文學》月刊,總第 303 期,2010 年 3 月,刊登簡介、9 首新詩〈凝〉〈淵泉〉〈所謂永恆〉〈懷舊〉〈流螢〉〈貓尾花〉〈秋暮〉〈月森林〉〈在那星星上〉及圖畫 1 幅,頁 76。

8.安徽省文聯主辦《安徽文學》,2010.02,發表新詩 2 首〈雲淡了,風清了〉〈縱。然剎那〉,頁 116。

9.天津市作家協會、天津日報報業集團主辦《天津文學》,

總第 471 期，2010 年 01 期，新詩 6 首〈星河〉〈颱風夜〉〈風雨之後〉〈夜祭〉〈七月〉〈海上的中秋〉，頁 95。

9-1. 《天津文學》，總第 483 期，2011 年 01 期，新詩發表 8 首〈在我深深的足跡上〉〈偶然的駐足〉〈畜欄的空洞聲〉〈秋日的港灣〉〈細密的雨聲〉〈林中小徑的黃昏〉〈我不嘆息、注視和嚮往〉〈夏荷〉，頁 92。

10.北京《文化中國》雜誌社主辦，《老年作家》季刊，主管：中國文化〈集團〉有限公司，2009 年第 4 期書評〈幸福的沉思─讀吳開晉《游心集》〉，頁 30-32，2009 年 12 月。

10-1. 《老年作家》2011 年第 1 期，總第 17 期，詩評〈簡論耿建華詩歌的意象藝術〉，頁 35-37，2011 年 3 月。

10-2. 《老年作家》2011 年第 2 期，總第 18 期，封面人物刊登林明理個人彩色照片及推薦，封底刊登作者水彩畫。

10-3. 《老年作家》2011 年第 3 期，總第 19 期，刊於封面後一頁─詩評〈讀吳開晉《游心集》〉，2011 年 9 月。

11. 北京《文化中國》雜誌社主辦，大連市《網絡作品》，2010 年第 3 期，刊作者簡介照片、書介及新詩 4 首〈正月的融雪〉〈紗帽山秋林〉〈在我深深的足跡上〉〈密林〉，頁 72，2010 年 6 月。

12 湖北省作協主辦《湖北作家》，2009 年秋季號，總第 32 期，頁 24-27，發表書評〈古遠清《台灣當代新詩史》的遺憾〉。

13.中國四川省巫山縣委宣傳部主辦《巫山》大型雙月刊，總第 7 期，2010 年 2 月發表詩 1 首〈夜思〉，頁 55。

13-1. 《巫山》大型雙月刊，總第 9 期，2010 年 4 月，刊登

彩色水彩畫作 1 幅〈水鄉〉。

14.山東省蘇東坡詩書畫院主辦《超然詩書畫》，2009.12 總
　第 1 期，刊作者簡介照片及新詩 3 首〈金池塘〉〈雨夜〉
　〈燈下憶師〉、水彩畫 6 幅彩色版，頁 34-35。

14-1. 山東《超然詩書畫》，2010.12，總第 2 期，刊水彩畫
　2 幅彩色版，頁 13。

14-2. 山東《超然詩書畫》，2011.12，總第 3 期，刊作者簡
　介照片、水彩畫彩色 2 幅及評論〈淺釋林莽的詩〈一條
　大江在無聲地流〉1 篇，頁 131-132。

14-3. 山東《超然詩書畫》，2012 年總第 4 期，刊作者簡介
　照片、彩色水彩畫 4 幅及評論〈由歐風到鄉愁─賀慕群
　繪畫中現代美初探〉1 篇，頁 177-179。

14-1.山東《超然》詩刊，總第 12 期 2009.12 詩 6 首畫 1 幅、
　13 期 2010.06 詩 4 首、15 期 2011.06 詩 2 首、17 期 2012.06
　詩 2 首詩評莫云一篇。2013.07 第 19 期刊登書畫評論〈畫
　牛大家─讀魯光《近墨者黑》〉、〈別具一格的大師
　── 試析沈鵬的詩〉、〈書藝不懈的追求者─夏順蔭〉
　三篇及作者得文藝獎章訊息。2013.12 總第 20 期刊登書
　評〈讀唐德亮的詩〉。

14-2.山東省《春芽兒童文學》，2013.06 創刊號刊登題詞新
　詩一首〈春芽〉，頁 11，書封底刊作者彩色水彩畫作一
　幅。

14-3.山東省春芽兒童文學研究會《春芽兒童文學》，2013.12，
　第 2 期，書封底刊登作者彩色水彩畫作一幅。

15.中國《黃河詩報》，2009 年 3 期，總第 5 期，發表詩 3
　首〈等候黎明〉〈雨夜〉〈瓶中信〉，頁 77。

16.山東省聊城市詩人協會主辦《魯西詩人》，2009 年.5 月，發表新詩 4 首〈草露〉〈大貝湖畔〉〈白色山脈〉〈黃昏雨〉，頁 42-43。

17.福建省文學藝術界聯合會主辦《台港文學選刊》，2008 年 9 月，發表詩 5 首〈雨夜〉〈金池塘〉〈遲來的春〉〈瓶中信〉〈夜櫻〉，2009 發表詩歌。

18.四川省重慶《中國微型詩萃》第二卷，香港天馬出版，2008 年 11 月，及重慶《中國微型詩》共發表詩〈朝露〉〈寒梅〉〈白楊〉〈夜霧〉〈動亂中的玫瑰〉〈三輪車夫〉〈風中的笛手〉〈蓮〉等 25 首詩。

19.北京市朝陽區文化館《芳草地》季刊，2012 年第 2 期，總第 48 期，刊登書評〈簡論《非馬藝術世界》的審美體驗〉，頁 50-57，刊物封面內頁刊登林明理水彩畫 1 幅彩色版〈郊外一景〉。

19-1. 北京市朝陽區文化館《芳草地》季刊，2013 年第 2 期，2013.06，總第 52 期，刊登書評《林莽詩歌藝術風格簡論》，頁 105-110。

20.遼寧省作協主辦《中國詩人》，2011 年第 5 卷，刊登〈生命的沉靜與奮發－淺釋白長鴻詩三首〉，頁 109-113。

21.福建福州市文聯主辦《海峽詩人》，第 2 期，2012.09，刊詩 3 首〈樹林入口〉〈回憶的沙漏〉〈懷舊〉，頁 30。

22.中國重慶南岸文聯、國際詩歌翻譯研究中心等主辦《世界詩人》季刊（混語版），總第 64 期，2011 年冬季號，書評〈清淡閑遠的歌者-讀許其正詩集《山不講話》〉，頁 53，書封面內頁刊登作者與非馬、許其正合影於第 30 屆世詩大會照片一張。

22-1.《世界詩人》季刊（混語版），2012 年 11 月，總第 68 期，書評〈簡論米蘭・里赫特《湖底活石》的自然美學思想，中英譯文刊登，頁 50-53，附作者簡介〈中英譯〉。

23.安徽省文學藝術界聯合會主辦，《詩歌月刊》，總第 136 期，2012 年 03 月，刊登作者簡介照片及詩 4 首〈九份黃昏〉〈九份之夜〉〈記夢〉〈生命的樹葉〉，頁 38-39。

23-1. 安徽省文學藝術界聯合會主辦，《詩歌月刊》，總第 157 期，2013 年 12 月，刊登新詩 7 首〈寄墾丁〉〈看灰面鵟鷹消逝〉〈冬日〉〈母親〉〈重生的喜悅〉〈雨，落在愛河的冬夜〉〈夕陽，驀地沉落了〉，刊作者簡介及彩色照片，頁 50-51。

24.香港《橄欖葉》詩報，2011 年 6 月第 1 期創刊號，刊登新詩 1 首〈在交織與遺落之間〉。2012 年 6 月第 3 期，刊登詩 1 首〈魯花樹〉。2012 年 12 月第 4 期，刊登新詩 2 首〈行經木棧道〉〈憶夢〉。2014 年 6 月第 7 期，刊登詩 1 首〈北風散步的小徑上〉。

25.廣東廣州《信息時報》2012.11.25C3 版刊登彭正雄：《歷代賢母事略》 書評 1 篇。

26.廣東省《清遠日報》，2012.08.10 閱讀版，刊登散文一篇〈《髻鬃花》的邂逅〉。

27.重慶市文史研究館《重慶藝苑》，2011 冬季號，刊登詩 2 首〈念故鄉〉〈夜之聲〉，頁 74-75。

28.廣東省《清遠日報》，2012.07.02，刊登書評〈我心中永恆的勇者塑像 ── 讀《古遠清這個人》〉。2012.8.10 刊〈《髻鬃花》的邂逅〉。

29.湖北省武漢市第一大報《長江日報》，2009 年 11 月 20

日，刊新詩 1 首〈原鄉—咏六堆〉。

30.河北省《新詩大觀》，總第 54 期，2009.02 刊詩 3 首〈春天〉〈黃昏雨〉〈大貝湖畔〉。

30-1.河北省《新詩大觀》，第 55 期，2009.04 刊詩 2 首〈霧裡的沙洲〉〈浪花〉。

30-2.河北省《新詩大觀》，第 56 期，2009.06 刊詩 6 首及作者簡介〈望鄉〉〈在秋山的頂上守候〉〈影子灑落愛丁堡上〉〈長巷〉〈塵緣〉〈送別〉。

31.安徽省《大別山詩刊》，主管單位：六安市委宣傳部，2012年總第 23 期，頁 72-73，刊登得「榮譽獎」新詩 1 首〈歌飛霍山茶鄉〉，收錄「霍山黃芽」杯全國原創詩歌大賽專刊，頁 72-73。

32.遼寧省盤錦市詩詞學會《盤錦詩詞》季刊，2009 年伍‧陸期，刊新詩 2 首〈想念的季節〉〈山茶〉，頁 96。2010年伍‧陸期，刊新詩 2 首〈細密的雨聲〉〈長虹橋畔〉頁 89。2011 年壹‧貳期，刊詩 1 首〈憂鬱〉頁 93。

33.黃中模等著，《兩岸詩星共月圓》，主辦：重慶師範大學，中國文聯出版社出版，
收錄林明理詩評 2 篇〈綠蒂《春天記事》的素描〉頁 118-125，〈評雪飛《歷史進行曲》〉頁 256-264。

34.遼寧省《凌雲詩刊》，總第 9 期，2010 年第 3 期，新詩 3首〈回到從前〉〈靜谷之憶〉〈三月的微風〉，頁 43。

35. 遼寧瑞州文學藝術學會主辦《瑞州文學》，2012.11 創刊號，刊登詩 2 首〈回到從前〉〈靜谷之憶〉及作者簡介，頁 79。

36.中國澳門《華文百花》，2013.01 期總第 18 期，2013.08

刊詩 4 首。

37.廣東省《西江日報》，2013.7.3，刊詩評 1 篇〈情繫瑤山
　　的生命樂章 —— 讀唐德亮的詩〉。

38.古遠清編著，《謝冕評說三十年》，海天出版社，2014.01
　　第一版，頁 279，收錄詩作一首〈北國的白樺 —— 致謝
　　冕教授〉。

39.老岱主編，《北都文藝》，2013 年第 2 期《海內外漢詩
　　專號》，刊登詩作 4 首。

40.蔡麗雙主編，《赤子情》，中國文聯出版社，2012.11 初
　　版，收錄詩一首〈海祭 —— 福爾摩莎〉，頁 307。

41.質貞編，《古遠清這個人》，香港文學報社出版，2011
　　年 8 月，頁 372-373，收錄作者簡介照片及評論〈我心
　　中永恆的勇者塑像〉。

42.《羊城晚報》，2009.10.15 刊新詩 1 首〈星河〉，B4 版。

43. 池州市杏花村中學〈杏花苑〉，第 15 期 2013.03，刊 2
　　新詩〈山寺前一隅〉〈墨菊〉。

44.《珞珈詩苑》〈十〉，武漢大學主辦，武漢大學珞珈詩社
　　協辦，2012.12，頁 171-173，刊古詩 4 首〈暮春〉〈默
　　喚〉〈湖山高秋〉〈秋盡〉及新詩 1 首〈沒有第二個拾
　　荒乞討婦〉。

45.由中國文藝協會與江蘇省淮安市淮陰區人民政府主辦的
　　第六屆「漂母杯」海峽兩岸母愛主題散文作品大賽於
　　2014.7 於淮安市頒獎，〈母親與我〉獲散文三等獎，
　　新詩〈母親〉獲二等獎。

46.遼寧省《燕山文學》，2014 年總第 2 期，頁 32，刊書
　　評〈夜讀斯聲的詩〉。

47."湘家蕩之戀"國際散文詩徵文獲榮譽獎,散文詩作品:〈寫給相湖的歌〉,嘉興市湘家蕩區域開發建設管理委員會、中外散文詩學會舉辦,2014.9.28 頒獎於湘家蕩。

48.四川省散文詩學會主辦《散文詩世界》,2014 年第 9 期,總第 113 期,刊得榮譽獎詩作〈寫給相湖的歌〉,頁 10。

49.吳開晉著,〈吳開晉詩文選〉〈上〉,北京,團結出版,2013.10 出版,收錄林明理詩評〈簡論吳開晉詩歌的藝術思維〉及〈幸福的沉思 —— 讀吳開晉《游心集》〉。

50.譚五昌教授主編,《國際漢語詩歌》,2013.11,北京,線裝書局出版,收錄林明理的新詩三首〈海頌〉〈北國的白樺-致北京大學謝冕教授〉〈歌飛阿里山森林〉及獲當選「國際漢語詩歌協會理事」〈2013-2016〉。

51.安徽省《大江詩壇 2014 中國詩選》收錄書評 1 篇〈從孤獨中開掘出詩藝之花 —— 淺釋《艾蜜莉·狄金生詩選》〉。

52.山西當代中國新詩研究所編,王立世主編《當代著名漢語詩人 詩書畫檔案》,北京,中國文聯出版社,2015.01出版,頁 208-209.收錄林明理新詩三首〈想念的季節〉〈在每個山水之間〉〈九份黃昏〉及水彩畫兩幅、作者簡介、個人照片。

53.湖南文聯《創作與評論》,2015 年 2 月號下半月,林明理著、王覓採訪整理,〈新詩是大陸與臺灣的彩虹橋〉。

●臺灣「國家圖書館」期刊

1.《國家圖書館館訊》特載,2009 年 11 月,發表書評 1 篇

〈讀王璞〈作家錄影傳記十年剪影〉新書有感〉，頁 7-9。

2.《全國新書資訊月刊》2010 年 3 月起至 2013 年 7 月，共發表詩評及書評共 26 篇。資料存藏於國家圖書館「期刊文獻資訊網」。

http://readopac1.ncl.edu.tw/nclserialFront/search/search_result.jsp?la=ch&relate=XXX&dtdId=000040&search_index=all&search_value=%E6%9E%97%E6%98%8E%E7%90%86%24&search_mode=

第 135 期書評讀丁文智〈花 也不全然開在春季〉，第 136 期詩評〈楊允達其人及其作品〉，138 期書評〈讀《廣域圖書館》── 兼述顧敏與圖書館管理的理論與實務〉，140 期詩評〈高曠清逸的詩境 ── 張默〉，142 期書評〈陳滿銘與《意象學廣論》研究述評〉，143 期書評〈試賞魯蛟的詩集《舞蹈》，144 期詩評〈商禽詩的意象表現〉，146 期詩評〈談周夢蝶詩與審美昇華〉，147 期詩評〈鄭愁予 ── 站在中西藝術匯合處的詩人〉，148 期詩評〈旅美詩人非馬及其作品〉，149 期書評〈淺釋隱地《風雲舞山》詩五首〉，150 期詩評〈淺釋鍾鼎文的詩〈雪蓮謠〉、〈三峽〉〉，151 期書評〈讀《高準游踪散紀》〉，152 期〈走過歲月 ── 臺灣文史哲出版社掠影〉，153 期詩評〈簡政珍詩歌藝術之管見〉，155 期詩評〈簡論郭楓和他的詩歌價值〉，156 期書評〈品蔡登山《讀人閱史》〉，158 期〈文津出版社邱鎮京教授掠影〉，159 期書評〈讀麥穗詩集《歌我泰雅》〉，160 期詩評〈楊牧詩歌的風格特質〉，161 期詩評〈王潤華和他的新詩創作研究〉，162 期書評《淺釋胡爾泰的詩》，164 期詩

評〈淺釋歐德嘉詩作三首〉，165 期詩評〈淺析林亨泰的詩歌藝術〉，171 期書評〈淺釋綠蒂《冬雪冰清》詩三首〉。175 期詩評〈簡論許達然詩的通感〉。

●臺灣學刊物

1. 佛光大學文學院中國歷史學會《史學集刊》，第 42 集，2010 年 10 月，發表書評〈概觀吳鈞《魯迅翻譯文學研究》有感〉，頁 231-240。

2. 佛光大學文學院中國歷史學會《史學集刊》，第 43 集，2011 年 12 月，發表書評〈評蔡輝振的《魯迅小說研究》，頁 181-189。

3. 真理大學臺灣文學資料館發行《臺灣文學評論》，2011 年 10 月，第 11 卷第 4 期，刊作者照及書評〈莫渝及其台語詩〉，頁 73-77。

3-1.《臺灣文學評論》，2012 年第 12 卷第 1 期，刊作者照及書評〈讀張德本《累世之靶》〉、〈讀李若鶯詩集《寫生》〉共 2 篇，頁 56-63。

3-2.《臺灣文學評論》，2012 年 4 月第 12 卷第 2 期書評刊作者照及書評〈吳德亮 —— 讀《台灣的茶園與茶館》〉，頁 90-93、新詩 1 首〈淡水紅毛城〉及作者簡介照片，頁 186-187。

3-3.《臺灣文學評論》，2012 年第 3 期，刊登作者照 3 張、新詩 3 首〈吉貝耍‧孝海祭〉〈森林深處〉〈憶夢〉，林明理畫作 1 幅，頁 184-187。

3-4.《臺灣文學評論》，2012 年第 4 期，2012 年 10 月，刊登評論〈淺談西川滿的文學思考〉，頁 76-82。

4. 真理大學人文學院台灣文學系彙編，第 16 屆台灣文學牛
   津獎暨《趙天儀文學學術研討會》論文集，2012 年 11
   月 24 日收錄詩評 1 篇〈趙天儀生態詩思想初步探究〉，
   頁 258-266。
5. 國立台灣文學館出版，《臺灣現當代作家研究資料彙編
   40 集 鄭愁予》，丁旭輝編選，收錄林明理撰文一篇〈鄭
   愁予：站在中西藝術匯合處的詩人〉，頁 217-221。

●臺灣詩文刊物報紙暨作品收錄

1.《創世紀》詩雜誌，160 期，2009.09 刊詩評〈讀須文蔚《橄
   仔樹》有感〉、〈周夢蝶的詩〈垂釣者〉的藝術直覺〉、
   〈解析大荒兩首詩〉、〈神木的塑像--魯蛟〉、〈「照
   夜白」的象徵--非馬〉〉、〈辛牧在台灣詩壇的意義〉6
   篇，161 期 2009.12 詩評 3 篇〈當代三家詩賞析 ── 洛夫、
   愚溪、方明〉。162 期 2010.03 刊詩〈流星雨〉，163 期
   2010.06 刊詩〈靜寂的黃昏〉及詩評〈淺釋楊允達的詩
   〈時間四題〉〉，164 期 2010.09 詩〈回憶的沙漏〉〈岸
   畔之樹〉及藝評〈解讀丁雄泉創作和美學的面向。165
   期 2010.12 刊詩〈一切都在理性的掌握中〉〈綠淵潭〉
   及詩評〈商禽詩的哲學沉思〉。166 期 2011.03 刊詩〈海
   祭〉〈山楂樹〉及藝評〈楊柏林詩與雕塑的審美體悟〉。
   167 期 2011.06 刊詩評〈淺釋碧果的詩三首〉，168 期
   2011.09 刊詩〈行經木棧道〉〈牽引〉〈在白色的夏季
   裡〉及詩評〈淺釋連水淼詩歌的藝術形象〉。169 期
   2011.12 刊詩〈記夢〉〈霧起的時候〉及詩評〈讀許水

富的詩〉，170 期 2012.03 刊詩〈在每個山水之間〉及
詩評〈讀汪啟疆詩筆抒豪情〉。171 期 2012.06 刊詩〈看
灰面鵟鷹消逝〉及〈評潘郁琦的詩〉，172 期 2012.09
書評〈讀方秀雲詩集〉。173 期 2012.12 刊詩〈雨，落
在愛河的冬季〉及詩評〈淺析紀弦詩五首〉，174 期
2013.03 詩評〈讀朵思的詩〉。

2. 《文訊雜誌》，第 291 期，2010 年 1 月，詩評鍾鼎文，
頁 24-26。

2-1.《文訊雜誌》，第 293 期，2010 年 3 月，詩評張默，頁
22-24。

2-2.《文訊雜誌》，第 297 期，2010 年 7 月，詩評愚溪，頁
18-19。

2-3.《文訊雜誌》，第 302 期，2010 年 12 月，書評張騰蛟《筆
花》，頁 118-119。

2-4.《文訊雜誌》，第 311 期，2011 年 09 月，書評雨弦《生
命的窗口》，頁 128-129。

2-5.《文訊雜誌》，第 316 期，2012 年 02 月，書評莫渝《走
入春雨》，頁 122-123。

2-6.《文訊雜誌》，第 330 期，2013 年 04 月，書評尹玲《故
事故事》，頁 138-139。

3.《笠》詩刊，2008 起，自第 263 期至 305 期 2015.02 止，
共發表詩 52 首、散文 3 篇及詩評 23 篇。

3-1.《笠》詩刊，263 期 2008.02 刊新詩〈丁香花開〉〈雨夜〉、
264 期 2008.04 刊詩〈塵緣〉〈螢光與飛蟲〉、265 期
2008.06 刊詩〈金池塘〉〈遲來的春天〉、266 期 2008.08
刊詩〈山問〉、268 期 2008.12 刊詩〈夜櫻〉〈寒松〉、

269 期 2009.02 刊詩〈長巷〉〈冬盡之後〉、270 期 2009.04
詩〈北極星〉〈愛是一種光亮〉〈往事〉、271 期 2009.06
詩〈夏荷〉〈小雨〉及詩評〈小論陳坤崙〉、272 期 2009.08
詩〈雲豹〉〈渡口〉〈夜，溜過原野〉及詩評〈讀莫渝
的詩〉、273 期 2009.10 詩〈颱風夜〉〈風雨之後〉〈夜
祭〉〈今夜，我走入一星燈火〉及詩評〈讀陳千武詩 4
首〉274 期 2009.12 詩〈傳說〉〈春草〉〈崖邊的流雲〉
及書評〈曾貴海詩集《湖濱沉思》〉。

3-2. 《笠》詩刊，277 期 2010.06 刊詩〈傾聽大海〉〈原鄉
　　 ── 咏六堆〉及詩評〈不凋的漂木 ── 薛柏谷的詩賞
　　 析〉、278 期 2010.08 散文〈愛情的巡禮〉及詩〈木框
　　 上的盆花〉、279 期 2010.10 詩〈聲音在瓦礫裡化為泣
　　 血〉、280 期 2010.12 詩〈行經河深處〉〈紗帽山秋林〉
　　 及詩評江自得、281 期 2011.02 詩〈在交織與遺落之間〉
　　 〈岸畔〉、282 期 2011.04 詩評〈淺析鄭烱明《三重奏》
　　 詩三首〉、283 期 2011.06 詩〈在雕刻室裡〉、284 期
　　 2011.08 詩評〈略論莫渝的詩風〉、286 期書評〈黃騰輝
　　 詩集《冬日歲月》賞析〉、287 期 2012.02 散文〈神遊
　　 薩摩亞藍湖〉及詩〈夜宿南灣〉、288 期 2012.04 詩〈如
　　 果你立在冬雪裡〉及詩評〈試析林豐明詩歌的意象力〉、
　　 289 期 2012.06 詩〈念故鄉〉〈思念的雨後〉及詩評岩
　　 上、290 期 2012.08 詩〈追悼 ── 陳千武前輩〉、291 期
　　 2012.10 詩評〈評陳坤崙的詩〉、293 期 2013.02 書評〈讀
　　 非馬詩集《蚱蜢世界》〉、294 期 2013.04 詩〈一個雨
　　 幕的清晨〉〈墨菊〉〈春芽〉及詩評〈讀吳俊賢的詩〉、
　　 295 期 2013.06 詩〈知本之夜〉〈回鄉〉及詩評〈讀李

昌憲的詩〉、296 期 2013.08 詩〈暮來的小溪〉〈我原鄉的欖仁樹〉及詩評〈讀林盛彬的詩〉、297 期詩〈釣魚台的天空〉及詩評〈讀王白淵的詩〉、298 期 2013.12 詩〈你繫著落日的漁光〉及書評〈讀莫渝《光之穹頂》〉。

3-3. 《笠》詩刊，299 期 2014.02 刊詩〈東隆宮街景〉、300 期 2014.04 刊詩評〈夜讀劉克襄詩數首〉，頁 165-170。301 期 2014.06 刊詩評〈讀李魁賢的詩〉及新詩 2 首〈憶友—Emesto Kahan〉〈富岡海堤小吟〉。302 期 2014.08 刊詩評〈讀羅浪的詩〉，頁 146-150。304 期 2014.12 刊詩評〈清純與哲思的交匯 ── 讀陳明克的詩〉。

3-4. 《笠》詩刊，305 期 2015.02 刊〈堅守與理想-讀葉迪的詩〉

4. 《文學臺灣》季刊，第 72 期，2009.10.冬季號，頁 81-82. 刊詩 2 首〈莫拉克颱風〉、〈夜祭 ── 紀念小林村夜祭而作〉。

4-1. 《文學臺灣》季刊，第 73 期，2010.01.春季號，頁 94. 刊詩 1 首〈光點〉。

4-2. 《文學臺灣》季刊，第 73 期，2010.01.春季號，頁 94. 刊詩 1 首〈光點〉。

4-3. 《文學臺灣》季刊，第 74 期，2010.04.夏季號，頁 131. 刊詩 1 首〈拂曉之前〉。

4-4. 《文學臺灣》季刊，第 75 期，2010.07.秋季號，頁 146. 刊詩 1 首〈回到從前〉。

4-5. 《文學臺灣》季刊，第 77 期，2011.01.春季號，頁 177. 刊詩 1 首〈遙寄商禽〉。

4-6. 《文學臺灣》季刊，第 78 期，2011.04.夏季號，頁 75. 刊詩 1 首〈在雕刻室裡〉。

4-7.《文學臺灣》季刊，第 79 期，2011.07.秋季號，頁 130. 刊詩 1 首〈九份黃昏〉。

4-8.《文學臺灣》季刊，第 83 期，2012.07.秋季號，頁 55. 刊詩 1 首〈吉貝耍・孝海祭〉。

4-9.《文學臺灣》季刊，第 85 期，2013.01.春季號，頁 79-80. 刊詩 1 首〈給司馬庫斯〉。

5.《人間福報》，2007 年至 2015 年 3 月止，共刊登新詩 76 首，散文、書畫評論、生命書寫、閱讀版、家庭版、投書等 54 篇及刊林明理繪畫作品 43 幅、攝影作品 7 件。

5-1.《人間福報》2007.2.22 刊生命書寫版〈親恩無限〉、2007.3.29 刊〈心轉境則轉〉、2007.4.1 刊〈山中冥想〉、2007.4.5 刊〈難忘婆媳情〉，2007.4.11 刊水彩畫作於副刊，2007.5.1 刊〈惜福惜緣〉、2007.5.4 刊〈康乃馨的祝福〉、2007.5.24 刊〈紅龜粿〉、2007.6.2 刊〈觀心自照〉、2007.6.15 刊〈黃金樹〉、2007.7.8 刊〈憶亡友〉，2007.7.13 刊詩〈愛的禮讚〉，2007.7.23〈生命裡的春天〉，2007.7.26 刊投書版〈夜晚愈熱，倡導生態建築〉、2007.7.27 刊〈水質惡化，政府渾然不察〉、2007.7.28 刊〈生技產業發展，刻不容緩〉，2007.7.31 刊生命書寫版〈生命故事的寫手〉、2007.8.4 投書版刊〈公投入聯 不利兩岸關係〉，2007.8.17 家庭版〈善待家人〉、2007.8.31〈爬山之樂〉、2007.9.11 刊家庭版〈家有妙老爹〉、2007.10.2 刊副刊水彩畫 1 幅，2007.10.10 刊〈緬懷旗津〉、2007.10.18 刊〈另類思考〉、2007.10.30 刊家庭版〈爸爸的勇氣〉、2007.11.9 刊〈看山吟水〉、2007.11.13 刊家庭版〈人生的考驗〉，2007.12.13 刊詩〈默喚〉。

5-2.《人間福報》2008.2.1 刊詩〈影子灑落愛丁堡上〉，2008.2.20 刊詩〈愛的實現〉、2008.4.10 刊詩〈金池塘〉、2008.4.22 刊詩〈倒影〉，2008.5.15 刊副刊散文〈聽雨，僧廬〉，2008.5.26 詩〈雲淡，風清了〉、2008.6.6 刊詩〈在秋山的頂上守候〉、2008.6.18 刊詩〈等候黎明〉、2008.7.10 刊詩〈山茶〉、2008.7.18 刊詩〈獨白〉、2008.7.31 刊詩〈航行者〉、2008.8.7 刊詩〈老紫藤〉、2008.8.26 刊詩〈水蓮〉、2008.9.11 刊詩〈可仍記得〉、2008.10.2 刊詩〈山雲〉、2008.10.20 刊詩〈簡靜是美〉、2008.11.3 刊散文〈燭光的躍動〉，2008.11.5 刊詩〈山間小路〉。

5-3.《人間福報》2009.1.16 詩〈北風〉、2009.2.2 詩〈冬望〉、2009.2.6 詩〈無言的讚美〉、2009.4.14 詩〈青藤花〉、2009.5.4 詩〈坐覺〉、2009.5.11 詩〈夏荷〉、2009.6.15 詩〈愛是一種光亮〉、2009.7.3 詩〈從海邊回來〉、2009.8.3 詩〈山桐花開時〉、2009.8.13 詩〈老樹〉、2009.8.21 詩〈風雨之後〉、2009.9.4 詩〈在初冬湖濱〉、2009.9.23 詩〈讀月〉、2009.10.5 詩〈海上的中秋〉、2009.10.22 詩〈聽雨〉、2009.10.26〈漁隱〉、2009.11.11 詩〈珍珠的水田〉，2009.11.15 刊生命書寫版〈平安就是福〉、2009.12.6 刊家庭版〈糖蛋的秘密〉，2009.12.18 刊詩〈在瀟瀟的雪夜〉。

5-4.《人間福報》2010.1.8 詩〈初冬一個訪客〉、2010.2.26 詩〈歲晚〉、2010.3.10 刊水彩畫作及詩〈墨竹〉、2010.3.31 刊彩畫作及詩〈想念的季節〉、2010.4.19 刊彩畫及詩〈四月的夜風〉、2010.5.2 刊生命書寫版〈難忘的畫面〉，2010.5.20 刊彩畫作及詩〈春已歸去〉、2010.7.7 刊彩畫

作及詩〈流螢〉，2010.7.23 副刊散文〈在我深深的足跡上〉，2010.9.21 刊彩色水彩畫作及詩〈光之湖〉、2010.11.15 刊彩色水彩畫作及詩〈月光〉。

5-5.《人間福報》2011.1.14 刊彩色水彩畫及詩〈靜海〉，2011.3.7 刊詩〈兩岸青山連天碧-陪海基會走過二十年感時〉，2011.3.8 散文〈古道尋幽〉、2011.4.11 刊水彩畫作及詩〈禪月〉、2011.5.23 副刊刊畫評〈高好禮的書畫藝術〉、2011.5.30 刊水彩畫及詩〈靜寂的黃昏〉、2011.7.12 刊彩色水彩畫作及詩〈春日的玉山〉、2011.9.12 刊水彩畫作及詩〈中秋懷想〉、2011.10.4 刊水彩畫作及詩〈山韻〉、2011.10.25 刊水彩畫作及詩〈夜之聲〉、2011.12.12 刊水彩畫及詩〈靜湖〉。

5-6.《人間福報》2012.1.31 刊副刊散文〈越野單車散紀〉，2012.5.22 副刊刊作者彩畫一幅，2012.6.5 刊水彩畫作及詩〈夕陽，驀地沉落了〉，2012.6.18 副刊刊作者照及散文〈卑南樂山的心影〉，2012.7.22 閱讀版刊書評〈讀《生活有書香》，2012.9.4 副刊刊詩〈永懷鍾鼎文老師〉及作者與鍾鼎文合照〉、2012.10.1 刊水彩畫作及詩〈沒有第二個拾荒乞討婦〉、2012.10.15 刊畫作及詩〈挺進吧，海上的男兒〉，2012.11.12 刊水彩畫作及詩〈給司馬庫斯〉、2012.12.3 刊攝影作 1 件及詩〈旗山老街的黃昏〉。

5-7.《人間福報》副刊 2013.1.1 刊水彩畫作及散文〈學佛之路〉，2013.1.7 刊水彩畫及詩〈冬憶-泰雅族祖靈祭〉，2012.7.23-7.24 刊副刊散文〈山裡的慈光〉〈上、下〉及作者照、水彩畫作，2013.1.29 副刊書評〈夜讀沈鵬詩〉及沈鵬、魯光贈書畫圖 2 張。2013.2.19 副刊刊水彩畫作

及散文《髻鬃花》的邂逅〉，2013.3.26 刊水彩畫及詩〈冬之雪〉，2013.4.30 刊水彩畫作及詩〈魯凱族黑米祭〉，2013.5.28 刊水彩畫作及詩〈母親〉，2013.6.16 閱讀版刊書評〈夜讀《成就的秘訣：金剛經》，2013.7.2 刊水彩畫作及詩〈月桃記憶〉，2013.7.8 副刊刊詩〈重生的喜悅〉，2013.8.12 刊詩〈曲冰橋上的吶喊〉，2013.9.16 副刊詩〈坐在秋陽下〉，2013.9.23 副刊詩評〈扎根於泥土的臺灣詩人：林煥彰〉。2013.11.18 刊詩〈海影〉。

5-8.《人間福報》副刊 2014.1.7 書評〈夜讀張騰蛟《書註》〉，2014.2.18 刊詩〈墾丁冬思〉，2014.5.13 副刊散文〈鞏伯伯的菜園子〉及水彩畫作。2014.6.5 副刊散文〈山居散記〉及水彩畫作。2014.6.30 副刊散文〈在匆匆一瞥間〉及水彩畫作。2014.7.16 刊投書版〈受國際尊重 要團結一致〉。2014.7.25 副刊散文〈初鹿牧場記遊〉及攝影作 3 張。2014.8.18 刊詩〈傷悼 —— 前鎮氣爆受難者〉及水彩畫作。2014.9.17 刊副刊散文〈都蘭紀行〉及攝影作 1 張、水彩畫 1 幅。2014.9.24 刊投書版〈人間處處有溫暖 詩人獻愛心 盼弱勢原住民重生〉。2014.10.6 刊副刊散文〈意外的訪客〉及水彩畫 1 幅。2014.10.24 副刊刊散文詩〈竹子湖之戀〉及水彩畫 1 幅。2014.11.14 副刊刊新詩〈無論是過去或現在〉及水彩畫 1 幅。2014.12.2 副刊刊新詩〈回鄉〉及水彩蠟筆畫 1 幅。

5-9.《人間福報》副刊 2015.1.23 刊副刊散文〈秋在花蓮〉，水彩畫 1 幅及攝影作品 2 張。2015.3.17 刊詩〈葛根塔拉草原之戀〉及水彩畫 1 幅。

6.《乾坤》詩刊，自 2010 年至 2014 年春季號，第 50 至 69

期，共發表新詩 43 首、古詩 4 首及詩評 14 篇。

6-1. 《乾坤》詩刊 50 期，2009 夏季號詩〈夏日長風〉〈江岸暮色〉〈來自大海的聲音〉〈風的默思〉，51 期，2009 秋封底刊作者照簡介詩觀及詩〈山桐花開時〉、52 期，2009 冬刊詩〈末日地窖〉及詩評尹玲，53 期，2010 春詩〈稻草人〉〈夜思〉及詩評辛鬱，54 期，2010 夏刊新詩〈大冠鷲的天空〉〈貓尾花〉〈霧〉及詩評向陽及舊詩 4 首〈暮春〉〈默喚〉〈湖山高秋〉〈秋盡〉，55 期，2010 秋刊新詩〈月橘〉〈芍藥〉〈馬櫻丹〉，56 期，2010 冬刊詩〈靜海〉〈因為愛〉及詩評徐世澤，57 期，刊中英譯詩〈十月秋雨〉〈星河〉及詩評鞏華，58 期，2011 夏詩評辛牧，59 期，2011 秋刊詩〈黎明時分〉〈雖已遠去〉及詩評錦連，60 期，2011 冬刊詩〈夜之聲〉〈我握你的手〉及詩評〈李瑞騰詩〈坎坷〉〈流浪狗〉的再解讀〉，61 期，2012 春詩評藍雲，62 期，2012 夏詩〈又是雨幕的清晨〉〈問愛〉及詩評〈一支臨風微擺的青蓮—淺釋莫云的詩〉，63 期，2012 秋刊詩〈玉山，我的母親〉〈秋之楓〉及詩評藍雲，64 期，2012 冬刊詩〈在積雪最深的時候〉及詩評楊宗翰，65 期，2013 春刊詩〈冬之雪〉〈詠車城〉，66 期，2013 夏刊詩〈追憶—鐵道詩人錦連〉，67 期，2013 秋刊詩評蘇紹連，69 期，2014 春刊書評〈讀丁文智詩集《重臨》隨感〉。

7. 《秋水》詩刊，136 期，2008.01 刊新詩〈松林中的風聲〉〈剪影〉、137 期 2008.04 詩〈林中漫步〉〈春雪飛紅〉、138 期 2008.07 詩〈煙雲〉、139 期 2008.10 詩〈露珠兒〉〈過客〉、140 期 2009.01 詩〈浪花〉〈夜思〉、141 期

2009.04 詩〈雨意〉〈清雨塘〉、142 期 2009.07 詩〈北窗下〉〈聽雨〉、143 期 2009.10 詩〈晚秋〉144 期 2010.1〈在瀟瀟的雪夜〉、145 期 2010.4 詩〈暮煙〉〈剪影〉、146 期 2010.07 詩〈在邊城〉〈懷舊〉、147 期 2010.10 書評〈讀張堃的《調色盤》〉、148 期 2011.01 書評〈夢幻詩境的行者 —— 淺釋《綠蒂詩選》〉、149 期 2011.04 詩〈林中小徑的黃昏〉〈枷鎖〉、150 期 2011.07 詩評〈淺釋屠岸的詩〈露臺下的等待〉〉、151 期 2011.11 詩評〈淺釋林錫嘉詩三首〉、152 期 2012.01 詩〈在寂靜蔭綠的雪道中〉、153 期 2012.04 詩評〈讀向明詩集《閒愁》〉、155 期 2012.10 詩〈秋林〉、156 期 2013.01〈靜寫生命的芬芳 —— 淺釋綠蒂詩二首〉。

7-1.《秋水》詩刊，161 期，2014.10，刊書評〈一隻優雅昂起的九色鹿 —— 讀梅爾的詩〉及新詩 2 首〈憶友 ——Kahan〉〈勇者的畫像-致綠蒂〉。162 期，2015.01 刊詩 2 首〈想妳，在墾丁〉、〈冬日神山部落〉。
《秋水》詩刊共發表詩 27 首及詩評 7 篇。

7-2.《戀戀秋水》秋水四十周年詩選，涂靜怡主編，2013.06 出版，收錄林明理詩 3 首〈煙雲〉〈在邊城〉〈懷舊〉，頁 186-187。

8.《海星》詩刊，2011 年 9 月創刊號，第 1 期，刊詩 2 首〈在蟲鳥唧唧鳴鳴的陽光裡〉〈雨後的夜晚〉，頁 52-53。

8-1.《海星》詩刊，2011 年 12 月，第 2 期，刊詩 4 首〈回到過去〉〈悼紐西蘭強震罹難者〉〈致貓頭鷹的故鄉〉〈來自珊瑚礁島的聲音〉頁 86-87，詩評 1 篇〈喬林詩歌的哲學意蘊〉頁 12-15。

8-2.《海星》詩刊，2012 年 3 月，第 3 期春季號，刊詩 4 首〈鐫痕〉〈在靜謐花香的路上〉〈惦念〉〈風滾草〉頁 94-95，詩評 1 篇〈風中銀樹碧　雨後天虹新 —— 淺釋鄭愁予的詩三首〉，頁 16-19。

8-3.《海星》詩刊，2012 年 6 月，第 4 期夏季號，刊詩詩評 1 篇〈引人注目的風景 —— 淺釋白萩的詩三首〉，頁 21-26。

8-4.《海星》詩刊，2012 年 9 月，第 5 期秋季號，刊詩 3 首〈海頌〉〈夏之吟〉〈夏至清晨〉頁 69，詩評 1 篇〈簡潔自然的藝術風韻-讀余光中的鄉土詩〉，頁 16-19。

8-5.《海星》詩刊，2012 年 12 月，第 6 期冬季號，刊作者畫封面彩色水彩畫、詩 2 首〈拂曉時刻〉〈默念〉頁 59，詩評 1 篇〈輕酌曉月賦詩葩 —— 讀羅智成《現代詩的 100 種可能》〉，頁 27-29。

8-6.《海星》詩刊，2012 年 12 月，第 6 期冬季號，刊作者畫封面彩色水彩畫、詩 2 首〈拂曉時刻〉〈默念〉頁 59，詩評 1 篇〈輕酌曉月賦詩葩 —— 讀羅智成《現代詩的 100 種可能》〉，頁 27-29。

8-7.《海星》詩刊，2013 年 3 月，第 7 期春季號，刊詩 1 首〈一如白樺樹〉，頁 102.詩評 1 篇〈遠離塵囂的清淨與自然-淺釋白靈的詩〉，頁 18-21。

8-8.《海星》詩刊，2013 年 6 月，第 8 期夏季號，刊詩 2 首〈歌飛阿里山森林〉〈老街吟〉頁 101，詩評 1 篇〈光明的歌者 —— 讀非馬《日光圍巾》〉，頁 14-17。

8-9.《海星》詩刊，2013 年 9 月，第 9 期秋季號，刊詩評 1 篇〈以詩為生命的苦吟者 —— 讀詹澈的詩〉，頁 18-21。

8-10.《海星》詩刊，2013 年 12 月，第 10 期冬季號，刊詩評 1 篇〈對純真美的藝術追求 ── 讀蕭蕭的詩〉，頁 16-19。

8-11.《海星》詩刊，2014 年 3 月，第 11 期春季號，刊詩評 1 篇〈抒情詩的創造性 ── 讀林文義的《旅人與戀人》〉，頁 16-19。

8-12.《海星》詩刊，2014.06，第 12 期夏季號，書評〈夜讀鍾玲詩集《霧在登山》，頁 15-19。

8-13.《海星》詩刊，2014.09，第 13 期秋季號，詩評〈走進周夢蝶的沉思歲月〉。

8-14.《海星》詩刊，2014.12，第 14 期冬季號，詩評〈夜讀莫云《夜之蠱》〉及詩〈那年冬夜〉。

8-15.《海星》詩刊，2015.03，第 15 期春季號，詩評〈陳義芝的浪漫與沉思〉及刊「翰墨詩香」詩書聯展參展活動照。

9. 臺南市政府文化局出版《鹽分地帶文學》雙月刊，第 37 期，2011 年 12 月，刊登詩 1 首〈越過這個秋季〉，頁 150。

9-1.《鹽分地帶文學》雙月刊，第 45 期，2013 年 4 月，刊登詩 1 首〈白河：蓮鄉之歌〉，頁 168。

10.鶴山 21 世紀國際論壇《新原人》雜誌季刊，第 70 期，2010 夏季號，發表詩 2 首〈懷鄉〉〈午夜〉，頁 152。

10-1.《新原人》季刊，2011 冬季號，第 76 期，書評 1 篇〈簡論米蘭・裏赫特《湖底活石》的自然美學思想，頁 214-220。

10-2.《新原人》季刊，2012 秋季號，第 79 期，詩評 1 篇〈伊利特凡・圖奇詩作及其價值〉，頁 228-231。

10-3.《新原人》季刊，2013 春季號，第 81 期，詩評〈一隻慨然高歌的靈鳥-讀普希金詩〉，頁 164-173，。

10-4.《新原人》季刊，2013 夏季號，第 82 期，〈中英譯〉書評伊利‧戴德切克著〈夜讀詩集《身後之物》，頁 150-160。

11.中國文藝協會會刊《文學人》季刊，革新版第 6 期 2009.08，畫評蔡友教授，頁 67-68.該畫評發表於佛光山，出席兩岸畫展研討會。

11-1.《文學人》季刊，革新版第 7 期 2009.11，刊詩 4 首〈原鄉- 詠六堆〉〈北埔夜歌〉〈風雨之後〉〈在我的眼睛深處〉，頁 104-105。

11-2.《文學人》季刊，革新版第 9 期，總 22 期，2010.12，刊詩評〈辛牧的詩化人生〉，頁 74-76。及新詩 2 首〈遙寄商禽〉〈破曉時分〉。

11-3.《文學人》季刊，革新版第 11 期 2013.05，刊作者獲 54 屆文藝獎章〈新詩類〉得獎名錄，頁 9。

12.《新地文學》季刊，第 18 期，2011.年 12 月，刊登詩 2 首〈九份之夜〉〈生命的樹葉〉，頁 54-55。

12-1.《新地文學》季刊，第 22 期，2012 年 12 月，刊登詩 2 首〈冬日〉〈詠車城〉，頁 172-173，及作者簡介。2012 年 12 月，第 22 期刊登詩 2 首。

13.高雄市《新文壇》季刊，自第 13 期至 2014 年 01 月，共發表詩 28 首，詩畫評論共 14 篇、畫作 3 幅。13 期 2009.1 刊新詩〈夜航〉〈湖山高秋〉、14 期 2009.04 刊詩〈冬之湖〉〈聽雨〉〈草露〉、15 期 2009.7 詩評辛牧及詩〈山桐花開時〉〈秋暮〉、16 期 2009.10 藝評〈非馬詩畫的審美體驗〉及詩〈致黃櫨樹〉〈春深〉〈光之湖〉、17 期 2010.1 詩〈雨中的綠意〉〈珍珠的水田〉、18 期

2010.04 散文〈真純的慈心─星雲大師〉及詩〈漁唱〉〈牧歸〉、19 期 2010.07 刊書封面水彩畫及封底作者簡介照片及詩評〈讀瘂弦〈歌〉〈瓶〉〉及詩〈停雲〉〈稻草人〉、20 期 2010.10 刊水彩畫及詩評謝明洲及詩〈秋日的港灣〉、21 期 2011.1 刊水彩畫及詩評〈淺釋吳鈞的詩四首〉及詩〈秋城夜雨─悼商禽〉〈昨夜下了一場雨〉、22 期 2011.4 詩評林莽及詩〈在清靜的茵綠裡〉、24 期 2011.07 畫評菜友及詩〈憂鬱〉、25 期 2011.10 書評馮馮、26 期 2012.1 詩評傅天虹及詩〈一棵雨中行的蕨樹〉、27 期 2012.4 書評楊奉琛及詩〈啊，卡地布〉、28 期 2012.7 刊書評〈略論陳義海的詩歌藝術〉及詩〈歌飛阿里山茶香〉、29 期 2012.10 詩〈當時間與地點都變了〉、30 期 2013.01 畫評賀慕群、31 期 2013.04 詩〈原鄉，詠撫順〉、32 期 2013.7 書評斯聲的詩、33 期 2013.10 詩評〈辛鬱的抒情詩印象〉及詩〈原鄉〉、34 期 2014.1 書評《讀楊濤詩集心窗》。

14. 高雄市《大海洋》詩雜誌，第 85 期，2012.07 刊登林明理簡介照片及英詩〈吳鈞譯〉4 首〈秋日的港灣〉〈海上的中秋〉〈海祭〉〈霧〉於頁 48-49、書評一篇〈試論《周世輔回憶錄》的文學價值〉，頁 50-51。

14-1.《大海洋》詩雜誌，第 86 期，2012.12 刊登林明理英詩 4 首〈吳鈞譯〉〈想念的季節〉〈樹林入口〉〈曾經〉〈十月秋雨〉於頁 20-21 及詩評一篇〈愛倫‧坡的詩化人生〉，頁 22-27。

14-2.《大海洋》詩雜誌，第 87 期，2013.07 刊登詩評 1 篇〈傑克‧斐外詩歌的意象藝術探微〉於頁 23-27 及獲第 54 屆

中國文藝獎章新詩類報導照片、證書資料於頁 22。

14-3.《大海洋》詩雜誌，第 88 期，2014.1 刊登詩評 1 篇〈一隻慨然高歌的靈鳥 —— 讀普希金的詩〉頁 26-31 及詩 1 首〈重生的喜悅〉於頁 26。

14-4.《大海洋》詩雜誌，第 89 期，2014.7 刊登詩評 1 篇〈評葦子的詩世界〉頁 74-76 及作者與 Prof.Kahan 諾貝爾和平獎得主合照一張。

14-5.《大海洋》詩雜誌，第 90 期，2015.01 刊登書評 1 篇〈從孤獨中開掘出詩藝之花 —— 淺釋《艾蜜莉‧狄金生詩選》〉，頁 120-124。

15.臺北市保安宮主辦，《大道季刊》第 62 期，2011 年 1 月，發表古蹟旅遊論述〈雨抹輕塵 清聲疏鐘 —— 觀臺北市大龍峒保安宮有感〉，頁 10-13。

16.《臺灣時報》，2011.12.16，臺灣文學版，刊登作者與丁旭輝等合照及散文 1 篇〈高應大「佛文盃」觀禮有感〉，頁 18。

16-1.《臺灣時報》，2013.6.3，臺灣文學版，刊登書評〈夜讀梁正宏《如果，轉九十度》〉，頁 18。

16-2.《臺灣時報》，2013.6.16，臺灣文學版，刊登詩評〈蓉子詩中的生命律動〉，頁 18。

16-3.《臺灣時報》，2013.7.4-7.5，臺灣文學版，刊登詩評〈林泠的抒情詩印象〉，頁 18。

16-4.《臺灣時報》，2013.8.5，臺灣文學版，刊登詩評〈走進路寒袖的詩世界〉，頁 21。

16-5.《臺灣時報》，臺灣文學版，刊登詩評 2013.8.18-8.19，臺灣文學版，刊登書評伊利‧戴德切克著〈夜讀詩集《身

後之物》，頁 21。

16-6.《臺灣時報》，臺灣文學版，2013.9.16，刊詩評印度前總統〈夜讀阿布杜‧卡藍詩〈我原鄉的欖仁樹〉，頁 21。

16-7.《臺灣時報》，臺灣文學版，2013.11.24，刊林明理的書序文〈在時光的倒影中〉及獲文學博士頒獎照，頁 21。

16-8.《臺灣時報》，臺灣文學版，2013.12.1-12.2 刊詩評〈淺析余光中的新詩三首〉，頁 21。

16-9.《臺灣時報》，臺灣文學版，2013.12.15-12.16 刊書評〈綠蒂詩歌的藝術成就及與綠蒂合照於馬來西亞 33 屆世詩大會參訪，頁 21。

16-10.《臺灣時報》，臺灣文學版，2014.5.4，刊散文 1 篇〈鞏伯伯的菜園子〉，水彩畫 1 幅及住家門前照，頁 21。

16-11.《臺灣時報》，臺灣文學版，2014.5.11-12，.刊登詩評〈關懷情 赤子心 ── 讀焦桐的詩〉，頁 21。

16-12.《臺灣時報》，臺灣文學版，2014.5.25 刊登詩評〈為故鄉而歌-讀陳黎的詩〉，頁 21。

16-13.《臺灣時報》，臺灣文學版，2014.8.15 刊登散文〈遷移記〉。

16-14.《臺灣時報》，臺灣文學版，2014.9.7-9/8 刊登詩評〈淺談羊令野的詩藝人生〉。

16-15.《臺灣時報》，臺灣文學版，2014.9.18 刊登新詩〈蘿蔔糕〉及攝影圖片 1 張。

16-16.《臺灣時報》，臺灣文學版，2014.10.12 刊登詩及水彩畫一幅〈流浪漢〉。

16-17.《臺灣時報》，臺灣文學版，2014.12.14-15 刊詩評〈堅守與理想 ── 讀葉笛的詩〉。

16-18.《臺灣時報》，臺灣文學版，2014.12.21-22 刊詩評〈讀
　　　吳晟的詩隨感〉。

16-19.《臺灣時報》，臺灣文學版，2015.1.4 刊書評〈讀傅予
　　　《籬笆外的歌聲》〉、與林明理合照一張。

16-20.《臺灣時報》，臺灣文學版，2015.1.11 刊〈縱浪翰墨
　　　詩香〉及林明理與隱地、向明、魯蛟合照 1 張。

16-21.《臺灣時報》，臺灣文學版，2015.2.1-2.2 刊詩評〈美
　　　麗的瞬間〉。

16-22.《臺灣時報》，臺灣文學版，2015.3.1 刊新詩 2 首〈四
　　　草湖中〉〈恬靜〉及攝影圖 1 幅。

17.《青年日報》副刊，2012.11.17，刊詩 1 首〈詠車城〉，
　　頁 10。

17-1.《青年日報》副刊，2012.12.16，刊詩 1 首〈寄墾丁〉，
　　　頁 10。

17-2.《青年日報》副刊，2013.3.9，刊詩 1 首〈野地〉，頁
　　　10。

17-3《青年日報》副刊，2013.4.4，刊詩 1 首〈祖靈祭〉，頁
　　　10。

18.《葡萄園》詩刊，第 177 期，2008 春季號刊詩〈瓶中信〉，
　　178 期 2008 夏季刊詩〈夜之海〉〈風吹的早晨〉〈送別〉
　　〈寒梅〉〈瓶中信〉，179 期 2008 秋詩〈追夢〉〈橄欖
　　花〉〈被遺忘的角落〉〈昨日已逝〉〈山雨滿樓〉〈可
　　仍記得〉，180 期 2008 冬刊詩〈靜夜〉〈春信〉〈夏日
　　涅瓦河畔〉〈行雲〉〈江晚〉〈日落〉，181 期散文〈重
　　遊台北城〉及詩〈星空中的風琴手〉〈墨竹〉〈春日江
　　中〉〈大貝湖畔〉〈一方寒影〉〈光點〉，182 期 2009

夏季詩〈流螢〉〈驀然回首〉〈木棉花道〉，183 期 2009
秋刊書評胡爾泰詩集及詩〈夢土的小溪〉〈秋暮〉〈岩
川之夜〉〈春已歸去〉，184 期 2009 冬刊書評〈讀吳開
晉《游心集》〉及詩〈七月〉〈西湖秋柳〉〈夢裡的山
谷〉。

19. 臺北《世界論壇報》，第 143 期至 168 期止，共刊登新詩
19 首，自傳文 1 篇。

19-1.《世界論壇報》，143 期新詩〈冬的洗禮〉〈沉默的湖
面〉〈我願是一片樹海〉、145 期 2008.11.20 詩〈考驗〉、
146 期 2008.12.4 詩〈想念的季節〉〈北窗下〉、147 期
2008.12.18〈望鄉〉〈翠堤偶思〉〈逗留〉、148 期 2009.1.8
詩〈看白梅花開〉〈又還丁香〉，149 期 2009.1.22 詩〈在
初冬湖濱〉，150 期詩〈春信〉，151 期 2009.3.5 詩〈老
街〉〈枯葉蝶〉及書介《夜櫻》。152 期 2009.3.19 詩〈萊
斯河向晚〉，153 期 2009.4.9 詩〈神農溪上的縴夫〉〈走
在彎曲的小徑上〉，157 期 2009.6.18 詩〈逗留〉，158
期 2009.7.9 詩〈墨竹〉〈萊斯河向晚〉，168 期 2009.12.10
詩〈驀然回首〉。

20. 臺南《台灣文學館》第 32 號，2011 年 9 月，頁 68，刊登
詩會合照。第 36 期，2012 年 09 月「榴紅詩會」詩人全
體合照 2 張紀念。

21. 第 30 屆世界詩人大會編印，Worid Poetry Anthology
2010・2010 世界詩選，2010 年 12 月 1-7 日，臺北，臺
灣。刊登簡介照片、中英譯詩 2 首〈雨夜〉〈夏荷〉，
頁 328-331 及論文 1 篇〈詩美的極致與藝術開拓〉〈中
英對照〉，吳鈞教授譯，頁 661-671。〈作者出席台北

吟誦譯詩及發表論文〉

21-1.第 33 屆世界詩人大會編印，33rd World Congress of poets，2013.10.25 刊登作者簡介照片及譯詩〈樹林入口〉〈Tree on the bank〉於頁 66。〈作者出席馬來西亞吟誦譯詩及領頒授文學博士證書〉

22.乾坤詩選〈2002-2011〉，《烙印的年痕》，林煥彰等編，收錄林明理詩〈末日地窖〉，頁 190-191，2011 年 12 月版。

23.葡萄園五十周年詩選，《半世紀之歌》，收錄〈瓶中信〉詩一首。2012 年 7 月版。

24.《詩人愛情社會學》，莫渝編，收錄林明理詩 1 首〈木框上的盆花〉，散文一篇〈愛情的巡禮〉。釀出版，頁 87-90，2011 年 6 月版。

25.《蚱蜢世界》，非馬著，2012 年 7 月秀威出版，版收錄林明理詩評非馬，頁 245-252。

26.《花也不全然開在春季》，丁文智著，爾雅 2009 年 12 月版，收錄林明理詩評〈鏡湖映碧峰 —— 讀丁文智的〈芒〉、〈自主〉〉一篇，頁 232-236。

26-1.《雪飛詩歌評論集》，雪飛著，2009 年海峽兩岸中秋詩歌朗誦會暨作品研討會論文，收錄林明理詩評 1 篇〈愛與美的洗禮-評雪飛《歷史進行曲〉，頁 129-140。

26-2.《光之穹頂》，莫渝著，高雄市文化局策畫出版，2013.10，收錄林明理書評〈真樸、意趣與悲憫 —— 讀莫渝《光之穹頂》〉。

27.《臺灣公論報》，2013.6.17，刊登詩 1 首〈生命的樹葉〉及林明理獲中國文藝獎章新詩類的報導照片。

28.《陳千武紀念文集》南投縣文化局出版，2014.05，收錄

林明理詩一首〈追悼 —— 陳千武前輩〉，頁 138。

29.《詩藝浩瀚》，中國詩歌藝術學會編，文史哲出版，2009
年 6 月，頁 339-348.刊簡介照片及新詩 8 首〈牧羊女的
晚禱〉〈夜櫻〉〈瓶中信〉〈金池塘〉〈遲來的春天〉
〈北極星〉〈雨夜〉〈寒松〉。

30.高雄市《太極拳雜誌》第 172 期 2007.8 刊〈習拳有感〉、
173 期 2007.10 刊散文〈古道之旅感言〉、174 期 2007.12
刊〈野薑花的回憶〉、〈生命的樂章〉及詩〈殘照〉。

30-1.第 237 期臺北《太極拳研究專輯》，2008.1.15 刊詩〈縱
然剎那〉。

31.「台灣詩學吹鼓吹詩論壇」網路推薦置頂 2007.10 詩〈青
煙〉、2007.11 詩〈夢橋〉、2007.12 詩〈秋收的黃昏〉、
2008.02 詩〈手心裡的束髮〉〈山影〉、2008.06 詩〈雨
中冥想〉。

32.《藝文論壇》創刊號 2009.5.4，中國詩歌藝術學會出版，
收錄林明理 1 文〈海峽兩岸兒童詩的發展方向〉，頁
98-99。第 2 期 2009.9.10 收錄書評〈評雪飛《歷史進行
曲》〉，頁 76-80。

33.張默編著，《小詩・隨身帖》，創世紀詩社出版，2014.9，
頁 21，收錄新詩〈流星雨〉1 首。

34.第三屆海峽兩岸漂母杯文學獎，《母愛，愛母》獲獎作品
集，刊登散文獎三等獎〈母親與我〉及新詩獎二等獎〈母
親〉，台北，聯經出版社，2014.10 出版。

35.莫渝著，《陽光與暗影》，新北市政府主辦，2014.10 出
版，收錄林明理書評〈讀莫渝《走入春雨》〉，頁 192-198。

●海外詩刊物及報紙

1. 美國《poems of the world》季刊，2010 年起至 2014 春季，發表非馬英譯林明理詩 2 首，吳鈞教授英譯林明理新詩 18 首。2010 春季號刊詩 1 首〈光點〉〈非馬譯〉，2010 夏刊詩 1 首〈夏荷〉，2010 秋刊詩 2 首〈十月秋雨〉〈雨夜〉，2010 冬刊詩 1 首〈流星雨〉，2011 春刊詩 1 首〈曾經〉，2011 夏刊詩 1 首〈所謂永恆〉，2011 秋刊詩 2 首〈想念的季節〉〈霧〉，2011 冬刊詩 1 首〈在那星星上〉，2012 春刊詩 1 首〈四月的夜風〉，2012 夏刊詩 1 首〈在白色的夏季裡〉。2012 秋刊詩〈秋日的港灣〉，2012 冬季刊詩 2 首〈午夜〉，〈流星雨〉。2013.春季刊詩〈看灰面鵟鷹消逝〉，2013.夏季刊詩〈早霧〉，2013 秋季刊詩〈秋復〉，2013 冬季刊詩〈海影〉，2014 春季刊詩〈Recalling of my Friend--Ernesto Kahan〉，2014 秋季號刊詩〈晚秋〉。

2. 美國報紙《亞特蘭大新聞》，2010 年 2 月起至 2011 年 7 月，共發表 9 篇文學評論及新詩 1 首〈偶然的佇足〉於 2010.8.6。2010.7.23 刊作者簡介照片及詩評〈商禽詩全集〉的哲學沉思〉、2010 年 7.30 刊作者簡介照片及詩評〈讀林煥彰的詩〈候鳥過境〉〉，2011 年 2 月 25 日刊簡介照片及詩畫評《葉光寒的美學思想》，2011.3.25 刊作者簡介照片及詩評〈讀涂靜怡的詩〉，2011.4.22 刊作者與古月合照及詩評〈古月的詩世界〉，2011.1.28 刊〈走向璀璨的遠景－曾淑賢以人性打造圖書館〉，2011.1.14 書評〈簡論非馬的散文創作 —— 讀《不為死貓寫悼歌》有感〉，2011.4.15 書評〈略論臺灣高準的詩才〉，

　　2011.3.4 刊簡介照片及書評〈評李浩的《評許廣平畫傳》
　　研究〉。2011.6.10 刊作者照及詩評〈鍾順文的《六點三
　　十六分》〉。

3. 美國《新大陸》雙月詩刊，任作者為名譽編委，2009 年
　　第 110 期迄 134 期止，共發表詩 45 首。第 117 期詩評葉
　　維廉、113 期詩評非馬共 2 篇。

4. 泰國《中華日報》，2009 年 8 月 11 日，刊登新詩 3 首〈笛
　　在深山中〉〈江岸暮色〉〈草露〉。

5. 馬尼拉出版，《世界日報》，2009.8.6，刊新詩 1 首〈夢
　　裡的山谷〉，頁 14。

　　●榮譽事項

1. 2013.10.21 獲美國世界文化藝術學院文學博士。

2. 獲 2011 年臺灣「國立高雄應用科技大學 詩歌類評審」
　　校長頒贈聘書。

3. 詩畫作品獲收入中國文聯 2015.01 出版「當代著名漢語
　　詩人詩書畫檔案」一書。

4. 2015.1.2 受邀訪談于重慶市研究生科研創新專案重點項
　　目「中國臺灣新詩生態調查及文體研究」，訪談內文刊
　　於湖南文聯《創作與評論》2015.02。

5. 獲《中國今世詩歌獎（2011-2012）指摘獎》第 7 名。

6. 獲 2013 年中國文藝協會與安徽省淮安市淮陰區人民政
　　府主辦，"漂母杯" 兩岸「母愛主題」散文大賽第三等
　　獎。2014 "漂母杯" 兩岸「母愛主題」散文大賽第三等
　　獎、詩歌第二等獎。

7. 新詩〈歌飛霍山茶鄉〉獲得安徽省「霍山黃茶」杯全國

原創詩歌大賽組委會「榮譽獎」榮譽證書。

8. 參加中國河南省開封市文學藝術聯合會「全國詠菊詩歌創作大賽」，榮獲銀獎證書〈2012.12.18 公告〉。

9. "湘家蕩之戀" 國際散文詩徵文獲榮譽獎，散文詩作品：〈寫給相湖的歌〉，嘉興市湘家蕩區域開發建設管理委員會、中外散文詩學會舉辦，2014.9.28 頒獎於湘家蕩。

10. 獲當選中國北京「國際漢語詩歌協會」理事〈2013-2016〉。

11. 2012 年 9 月 9 日人間衛視『知道』節目專訪林明理 1 小時，播出於第 110 集「以詩與畫追夢的心 —— 林明理」。

後　記

　　本書選取 112 首新詩作品，由吳鈞教授直接譯成英文。另附錄 10 首新作及由 1985 年諾貝爾和平獎得主 prof.kahan 教授寄贈譯詩。

　　出版前得到了山東大學吳開晉教授及美國著名詩人非馬〈馬為義博士〉惠賜祝賀詩詞，特此致謝。此外，也感謝臺灣「國圖」館長曾淑賢博士及海內外各刊物主編的支持。特別是南京師範大學吳錦教授、莆田學院彭文宇教授、華中師範大學鄒建軍教授、安徽師範大學王世華教授、鹽城師範學院薛家寶校長、陳義海教授、郭錫健教授、商丘師範學院高建立教授、內蒙古集寧師院田智校長、寧夏師範學院方建春教授、吳思敬教授、謝冕教授、古遠清教授、譚五昌教授、傅天虹教授、王珂教授、莊偉傑教授、黃中模教授、丁旭輝教授、文協綠蒂理事長、楊濤主編、莫云主編、朱學恕主編、人間福報副刊時雍、臺灣時報黃耀寬主編等等詩友的愛護。最後僅向文史哲出版社發行人彭正雄先生為本書所付出的辛勞致意。